D0848748

ASPECTS OF GREEK AND ROMAN LIFE

General Editor : H. H. Scullard

★　★　★

TRAJAN'S COLUMN AND THE DACIAN WARS

Lino Rossi

TRAJAN'S COLUMN AND THE DACIAN WARS

Lino Rossi

English translation revised by
J. M. C. Toynbee

CORNELL UNIVERSITY PRESS
ITHACA, NEW YORK

First published 1971

International Standard Book Number 0–8014–0594–7

Library of Congress Catalog Card Number 70–127778

PRINTED IN ENGLAND

CONTENTS

LIST OF ILLUSTRATIONS

FIGURES

FOREWORD

Trajan's Column is one of the most familiar, most spectacular, and best preserved monuments of ancient Rome. It has formed the subject of several large and learned German monographs, of a similar Italian monograph, and of a number of smaller books and articles in French, German, and Italian. It finds a conspicuous place in histories of Roman art written in various languages; and important papers in English periodicals have dealt in detail with some of the historical, topographical, and military problems raised by the sculptured reliefs, depicting Trajan's Dacian wars, that wind in a mighty spiral round its shaft. But in the present work we have the first English book wholly devoted to the Column and presenting it in a handy and richly illustrated volume that can both be read at ease at home and accompany the traveller to Rome. It is a book that the student and general reader will enjoy; and the specialist will find in it not a little that is new to him.

Dr Rossi is a distinguished Milanese pathologist, whose parergon is the study of warfare, chiefly ancient Roman and modern warfare. His approach to the Column's reliefs is, there-fore, first and foremost a military one. These reliefs were, of course, in part designed to enhance Trajan's personal renown. But to Dr Rossi they are, above all, a magnificent commemora-tion of the Roman army's achievements, with the emperor as comrade and leader: they are essentially an epic of all members, in all capacities, of the imperial forces – the most impressive armed forces put into the field until recent times. He outlines, from the military point of view, the background, in politics and in geography, against which the wars were planned; and he provides us with all the data that we need for understanding the organization, conditions of service, arms, armour, and other equipment of the men whose activities we follow on the sculptured frieze. The background, terrain, arms, dress, and other customs of the Dacian foe, as depicted in the sculptures and on coin-types relating to the wars, are also vividly described. Of special interest is Dr Rossi's method of identifying on the Column the units of Trajan's army by a careful appreciation of the conventions used for distinguishing both them and the tasks assigned to them; and here the study of shield-emblems plays a valuable part. Important, too, is the contrast that he draws between the more official, courtly, and conventional rendering of the wars on the Roman monument and the provincial panels that portray the self-same wars, very crudely, but often with greater fidelity to detail, from the Tropaeum Traiani at Adamklissi in Dobruja.

In Chapter VIII, the last and longest in the book, we have a running commentary on the author's photographs of the entire sequence of the scenes from the bottom to the top of the Column's shaft. Here Dr Rossi's special knowledge of the topography of one-time Dacia, and of the Dacian fortified sites that the Rumanian archaeologists have brought to light, is most illuminating. The reliefs may leave us in doubt as to the identity of a number of the incidents and places represented. But they form a coherent whole and display the story of the wars in an order of events and against a shifting landscape and architectural back-drop that we may reasonably take to be generally faithful to reality, so far as our meagre literary sources, and the actual geography and natural features of the war-theatre, make it possible to judge.

J. M. C. Toynbee

PREFACE

I WOULD LIKE to express my deepest gratitude to J. M. C. Toynbee (Laurence Professor Emerita of Classical Archaeology, Cambridge) for her generous advice, encouragement and invaluable help throughout the writing of this book. My thanks are also due to Professor F. B. Florescu (the Academy of Rumania) and to Professors Costantin and Hadrian Daicoviciu (the University of Cluj) who kindly supplied important material for study and illustration, as well as to Professor J. M. Hemelrijk (University of Amsterdam), the late Dr H. R. Wiedemer (Vindonissa Museum, Brugg), Dr D. Baatz (Saalburgmuseum, Bad-Homburg), Dr P. Cornaggia Medici (Milan) and Dr R. Riva (Gallarate) for help in collecting useful data on the Roman army. For their most expert and patient assistance, I would like to thank Thames and Hudson Ltd and, in particular, Mr Jamie Camplin, together with Professor H. H. Scullard, the general editor of the series. Finally, I gratefully record my wife's help in making the translation and in secretarial work.

L. R.

1 Trajan's Column amid the ruin of the arcades of the Basilica Ulpia in Trajan's Forum.

INTRODUCTION

The Column

Trajan's Column is 100 feet high, and is composed of 17 superimposed marble drums. Its pedestal is a square cube, measuring 17 feet on each of its sides, in one of which is a small door leading into the chamber that contained the golden cinerary urns of Trajan and his wife Plotina. Inside the Column's shaft a staircase, lit by 43 small windows, ascends to the top, which was once adorned with a gilt bronze statue of the emperor, now replaced by a statue of St Peter. The Column's outer surface takes the form of a ribbon, about 3 feet wide and 670 feet long, twisted round it in 23 spirals. The spirals cover 400 slabs and are carved with reliefs containing more than 2,500 figures. The square slabs of the base are also sculptured so as to represent a huge pile of arms and armour. A laurel wreath, interposed between shaft and pedestal, forms the torus of the Column.

4

33-4

The monument was put up in Trajan's new Forum behind the Basilica Ulpia and the later Templum Divi Traiani. It stood in a colonnaded court which was flanked by two libraries, one for Greek, the other for Latin books; from the windows of these buildings Romans could no doubt appreciate the Column's frieze in a way now no longer possible to the modern viewer who faces an isolated monument which towers high above him. The Column was dedicated to the emperor in AD 113; the dedicatory inscription above the door (see p. 49) appears to indicate that its purpose was to show the height of the cutting-back of the eastern shoulder of the Quirinal Hill which the construction of the new Forum required, while the use of the word *opera* may suggest not only such operations but also hint at imperial achievements in general.

The Column was intended to be a triumphal monument (a trophy), a memorial to the emperor's glory *(Virtus Augusti)*,

13

illustrating the great wars won by Trajan's army against the peoples of Dacia. Its future use as a funerary monument was not, it seems, part of the original conception.

As a result of the enduring admiration and respect evoked by this wonderful masterpiece, the Column has stood, untouched for nearly nineteen centuries, at the very centre of the Roman world amid the utter ruin of the surrounding Fora.

The frieze is a scroll, or *volumen*, an illustrated commemorative record that ought to be studied and understood as a whole; it should not be seen as a series of individual topics, isolated from their context. The purpose of the present book is to try to supply a reliable account of it as a document in pictures. The text and the reproduction of the entire frieze will be preceded by a sketch of the pictures' historical and geographical setting, together with the necessary facts concerning the Roman armed forces in Trajan's time and their Dacian opponents. Most of the photographs have been taken with a telecamera in full daylight from the original, in order to show the frieze as it appears to the observer on the spot with the aid of ordinary field glasses. Larger reproductions, taken from casts, have been added whenever necessary to bring out the finer details.

The Column as history in pictures

It could be said with truth that the Column is 'rare' in art but 'unique' in history, since it represents the only detailed documentation that we possess of Trajan's Dacian wars, events of outstanding importance which took place when Roman military power had reached its peak. The written sources for these wars are, in fact, almost totally lost. One line alone survives of Trajan's own report *(commentarii)*, while the few pages from Dio Cassius' history in Xiphilinus' abstract are very poor and confused (Dio, LXVIII; see Appendix A).

It must be borne in mind, first, that the sculptured frieze was designed according to the current rules of commemorative art. Thus personages and objects are reproduced with great attention to realistic detail and placed in the positions and associations conventionally adopted for suggesting abstract ideas. They are not merely parts of factual pictures. For the same reason, emphasis is laid upon some particular features and circumstances, while others are apparently toned down or even

2 The Emperor Trajan, young and strong, wearing a moulded cuirass and kilt adorned with motifs that probably refer to the outset of the Dacian campaign. There are a hexagonal shield (a type peculiar to the Germans in commemorative art), the Roman eagle and she-wolf, the helmeted Mars and the elephant head (denoting *aeternitas, munificentia*).

omitted. So, the events of the Dacian campaigns, and their presentation in the terms of a triumph, running from the bottom to the top of the spiral band, will be perceived by the onlooker once he is able, as was his predecessor in Roman times, to pick up the clue of the conventional meanings originally attached to the figures, to their inter-relationships and attitudes. A commemorative language of this kind was, in fact, highly developed and widely employed by the Romans in official representation on coins and public monuments: it was a picture-language that anybody, anywhere and at anytime could understand.

Today, our eyes and minds are accustomed to the modern picture-language of the cinema; and we should not therefore find it difficult to watch the sequence of scenes on the marble scroll as though it were a film-roll, unwound nineteen centuries ago.

Persons, animals, costumes, arms, standards, and ships are here accurately displayed against a background of forts, tents, huts, buildings, and harbours, all shown in bird's-eye view perspective and within a contracted landscape of rivers,

3 Far left, the dedication to Trajan, inscribed on a great slab on the Column's pedestal.

4, 5 Left, Trajan's Column today; and below, a condensed but realistic rendering of it as it originally appeared, on the reverse of a Trajanic *denarius* (BMC 454); the small doorway and dedicatory *tabula* above it are reproduced at the base, as well as the railing round at the top around the emperor's statue. The spiral with its relief is summarily indicated on the die.

mountains, bridges, and trees. The reliefs were once painted in realistic tints and details of armour and equipment were added in metal. Moreover, the pictures are so linked together that they suggest a continuous story, with only one sharp demarcation in the middle of the roll to separate the first from the second *69–70* Dacian war. Nevertheless, single scenes (about 3 × 5 feet wide) are distinguished from one another by the interposition of such vertical framing elements as a tree, a standing man, or the corner of a building, each part of the picture itself, or by a sudden change in the background or in the action.

At first sight one receives the impression of a lack of naturalism, owing to the disproportion between actors and scenery and the sudden changes of subject. But in order to understand these things one must get them into the right focus and adjust them to the following principles:

TIME: The succession of the scenes corresponds to the chronological order of events. From below upwards, anticlockwise, what comes before in place also happened earlier in time, and *33, 20, 102* vice versa. Night, weather and seasons are also hinted at.

SPACE: The direction of the gaze, gestures and movements of the figures indicates the actual orientation of the action concerned. Facing forward stands for going east or north-east (in the direction of Dacia, or downstream on the Danube), while facing backwards means going west or south-west (in the direction of Roman territory or upstream on the Danube).

CONVENTION AND SYMBOLS: In a method of representation as concise as that used on the Column one soldier or a single standard may stand for an entire unit, one tree for a wood, one hut for a village and so on. Different soldiers or standard-bearers, or several trees, or various buildings grouped together could stand for whole armies, forests, and towns, respectively. Permanent or temporary Roman camps *(castra, castella)* are identifiable from the type of material employed for their construction and from the different types of tents and pavilions inside. Other details and symbols, leading to the identification of many other elements, will be taken into consideration later, and the original colours (now vanished) must have provided further aids to exact recognition.

In this way it becomes possible to detect not only who the personages are, but also what they are doing and the where, when, how, and even why, of their activities. This is quite an amazing achievement, on a stone band only three feet wide.

Moving personages, actual objects, recognizable sites and realistic timing, all taken together, make up a true film, the direction of which is to be attributed to Apollodorus of Damascus, Trajan's architect. Like a modern director, he skilfully mastered the original script, derived from the reports and sketches of Trajan's war correspondents (and probably from Trajan's own *commentarii*), so as to distribute at the right place and in the right order scenes of war and peace, of hatred of the foe, of religious observance, of life and death in the world of Roman warfare.

Although he had to pay the most careful attention to the many details and rules of official commemoration, he succeeded in presenting the story in a broader epic guise. The skill and might of the Roman *exercitus*, based on the unity of its varied forces under the vitally important guidance of the emperor, its craftmanship in making preparations for battle, and its bravery in the actual conflict seem to convey, as the story proceeds step by step, the essential superiority and the inevitable victory of Rome. The Dacian foe, while treated with respect for his courage and self-sacrifice, exhibits only haste, rage, and the desperate strength of the barbarian.

But a touch of humanity has been subtly and deliberately introduced here and there into this vivid picture of power and triumph, rendering it as meaningful to the ordinary mortal as to the glorious emperor. For instance, the fickle fortunes of men in war are clearly suggested by juxtaposing sharply contrasted episodes, again a technique found in a modern moving picture: a scene with happy soldiers being granted gifts by Trajan is immediately followed by one of the humiliation and death of naked Roman prisoners, tortured by Dacian women. *40–1*

Anyone eager to enjoy the art, explore the history and experience the life of imperial Rome, should see, read and feel the wonders of Trajan's Column. It is the author's hope that the present book may be of some help in the endeavour to do this.

NOTE: Italicized marginal references indicate the scenes of the Column which are illustrated in sequence in Chapter VIII, pages 131–212.

CHAPTER I

TRAJAN'S DACIAN WARS

The historical situation

By the end of the first century AD the military power and the civil evolution of Rome had reached their climax. The fortified frontier *(limes)* of the empire in continental Europe extended from the Lower Rhine to the Black Sea, running for about 1500

Fig. i miles along the right bank of the Danube. The *limes* left the course of the Rhine near the modern Vinxtbach *(Finis)* to penetrate, eastwards, the Taunus forest and then to bend southwards for about 120 miles, at a point not far from Frankfurt. It then resumed its eastbound course, reaching the Danube near Eining, and thence followed the right river-bank as far as the Dobruja of today. The Danube was not only the strongest frontier barrier, but also represented a vital means of communication since it was linked with a network of military roads, thus ensuring cover and supplies for the army and the possibility of the further expansion of the imperial *limes* itself.

    The illustrated history on the Column is centred upon Dacia,

Fig. ii a fairly large territory beyond the middle course of the Danube (a part of present Rumania), which was inhabited by a population of Thracian stock (northern Thracians), with German and Sarmato-Scythian components. Thus Dacia embraced most of the modern Transylvania, Banat, and Valachia, and was bisected by the south-western Carpathian chains (Transylvanian Alps). The Dacians, owing to their geographical position and ethnic composition, had been substantially influenced by the Greek and Persian civilizations, and they had also kept up a close connection with the Roman world. The term 'barbarians', which the Romans used so glibly of under-privileged populations abroad, seems to be hardly suitable as applied to the Dacians. For while great national (or tribal) pride and individual gallantry in war were far from uncommon among the barbarian opponents of Rome, in the case of the Dacians

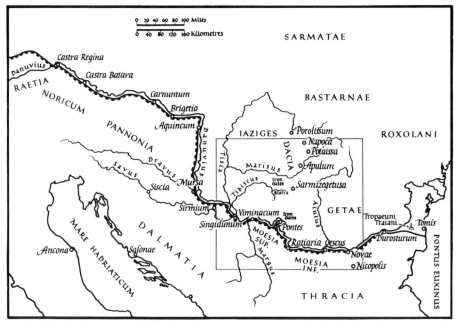

Fig. i The frontier of the Roman Empire in Western Europe. In Trajan's time the fortified frontier (*limes*) in continental Europe ran for about 1,500 miles along the right bank of the Danube. Within the square is the theatre of Trajan's Dacian wars (see *Fig. ii*, page 26–7).

these native virtues were combined with comparatively efficient organization and an eagerness to assimilate more advanced techniques and customs.

Economically, the Dacians seem to have been quite well-off (they engaged in agriculture, stock-breeding, and mining, gold included). As far as religion was concerned, they worshipped the god Zamolxis (or Zalmoxis), practised orgiastic and secret rites (including human sacrifice), and firmly believed in a heavenly life as a reward for the heroes who died for their country. Death was, then, willingly encountered by Dacian warriors who refused to surrender, even resorting to individual or mass suicides. Scenes of this kind can be seen on the Column, *137, 144* and they demonstrate the extremes of courage and resolution with which the Roman army was faced while campaigning in Dacia.

Such a strong and determined neighbour as Dacia could not but represent a grave danger to Rome. The threat to the Danubian *limes* had long become constant, since Dacian bands often crossed the river to raid and pillage the Roman provinces of Pannonia and Moesia beyond. Two punitive expeditions attempted by Domitian (AD 85–7) against the Dacians had both ended in utter disaster. Both the army of Oppius Sabinus, legate of Lower Moesia, and that of Cornelius Fuscus, praetorian prefect, had suffered devastating casualties, including their commanders. It also seems that an entire legion *(V Alaudae)* was lost with Fuscus. Even a local success of the Romans in Dacian territory, achieved in AD 88 by Tettius Julianus, was far from enabling Rome to wipe out the harm done to Roman military power and prestige on the Danubian frontier. As the conditions for a truce with the Dacians Rome was forced to pay them large sums of money and to hand over to her former enemy a number of military technicians and engineers. This latter condition proved particularly disastrous, in as much as these skilled Roman master-craftsmen, together with the numerous deserters from Roman units that had settled in Dacia, were to build up a Dacian army equipped and organized on the Roman model and unmatched in the 'barbarian' world until the misfortune of war overtook it.

Such was the complex and dangerous situation that faced Trajan on his assumption of imperial powers (AD 98); and soon realizing that diplomacy was not likely to solve the problem, he decided to make war against the Dacians. This was, of course, an extremely grave decision for many reasons. But in implementing it Trajan displayed those outstanding qualities of military commander and organizer, of political leader and economic planner which made him a great, perhaps the greatest Roman emperor.

The Dacians, in their turn, in conjunction with related and allied peoples, in chief the Bastarnae (of German stock) and the Roxolani (of Sarmato-Scythian stock), mustered a large army partly equipped and trained in the Roman way, but employing very special and heavy forms of armament, namely the battle-scythe used by the infantry and the complete suits of armour worn by the cavalry. The Dacian warriors were, moreover, masters of their own territory (little known to the Romans), which was rich in steep hills, thick woods and rapid rivers. The

6 A high-ranking Dacian (probably Decebalus himself) surrounded by other cap-wearing chieftains (*pilleati*) and by bare-headed, hairy commoners (*comati*), in a stone-walled citadel.

most impenetrable mountains had been fortified and turned into strongholds. A terrain of this kind would appear at first *58–64* sight to be very unsuitable for the operations of the Roman army with its classic battle-deployment of the legionary heavy infantry for fighting on open ground. Decebalus, the able and 6 gallant king of the Dacians, who had been long acquainted with the Romans both in war and in peace, was well aware of all this.

23

7 Trajan's road at the foot of the cliffs in the gorge of the Iron Gates of Orsova.

Trajan, on his side, had to concentrate a large number of units along a limited tract of the Danubian borderline, to build up an expeditionary force large enough for the heavy task before it, and to guarantee its liaisons with, and supplies from, the frontier bases, wherein enormous amounts of food and equipment had to be stored. Once across the Danube the Roman forces faced the danger of being cut off from their bases if the bridging was not done properly and if the crossing points were not defended; and the river in this sector is more than half a mile wide. Yet the network of roads along the Roman riverbank should have been sufficient to allow the speedy transit of convoys and troops to and from the bridges thrown across the Danube and thence to the expeditionary corps in Dacia. Moreover, at one point the Danube in fact narrows into a gorge, the so-called Iron Gates of Orsova.

Figs. ii, iii

Trajan undertook the enterprise with a clear mind and sure hand, employing methods and techniques so powerful and efficient that they still impress the modern student of military history.

24

8 The road cut into the cliffs along the Danube by Trajan's engineers was widened by cantilevered planks, supported on wooden beams which were inserted into the holes visible in the photograph.

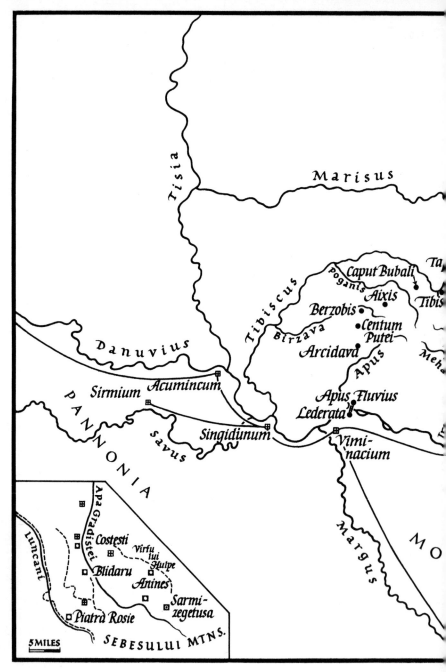

Fig. ii The theatre of Trajan's Dacian wars. This map corresponds to the square in *Fig. i* and has at its centre the hilly stronghold of the Transylvanian Alps. Within the outlined pentagon (enlarged at lower left) there is the Dacian

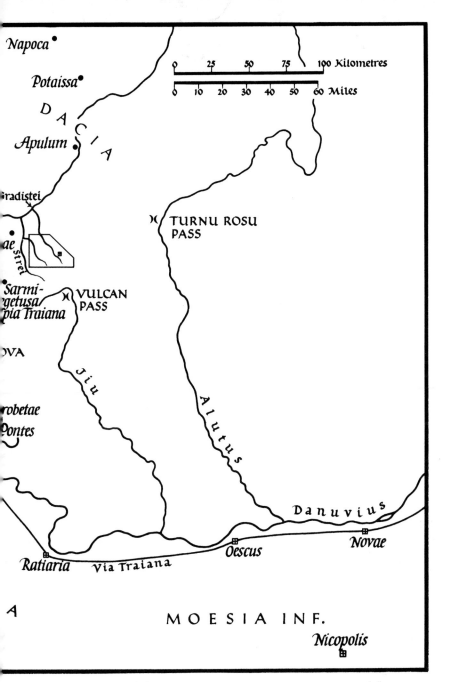

Napoca •

Potaissa •

D A C I A

Apulum •

Gradistei

ae

Strei

Sarmi-
getusa
pia Traiana

VULCAN
PASS

VA

TURNU ROSU
PASS

robetae

Pontes

Jiu

Alutus

Danuvius

Ratiaria   Via Traiana   Oescus   Novae

MOESIA INF.

Nicopolis

A

| 0 | 25 | 50 | 75 | 100 Kilometres |

| 0 | 10 | 20 | 30 | 40 | 50 | 60 Miles |

capital, Sarmizegetusa, situated at the bottom of the Apa Gradistei valley and
protected by a belt of hill-forts. Here circles in squares indicate Dacian hill-
forts, squares with a cross Roman camps, and dash-lines Dacian roads.

After a personal survey of the situation (AD 98–9), Trajan ordered two barge-bridges to be thrown across the Danube, up-
and downstream from the Iron Gates. Later he was to appoint

Fig. iii

89

After a personal survey of the situation (AD 98–9), Trajan ordered two barge-bridges to be thrown across the Danube, up- and downstream from the Iron Gates. Later he was to appoint Apollodorus of Damascus to build the longest permanent bridge of antiquity, with twenty pillars in masonry and wooden super-structures, in place of one of the bridges of barges.

With a view to improving the road approaches to, and the communications between, the two main crossings, Trajan also ordered a twelve miles stretch of road to be cut in the rocky Moesian bank of the Danube's gorge. Then the fleets of Pannonia and Moesia were summoned for the transport of troops and supplies (from north and south respectively).

The army which was concentrated in the area had been selected to face the strategic and tactical demands of a mobile war on rough and fortified territory. Furthermore, Trajan foresaw the vast possibilities offered by the employment of the *auxilia*. Hence, in support of an experienced group of legions, he mustered a very large number of auxiliary cavalry and infantry units, often equipped with special arms (archers, slingers, etc.), together with the *symmachiarii*, semi-regular bodies of barbarians which now make their first official entry into the Roman army. This great army, probably 100,000 men strong, will be considered in detail later, when we examine the spectacular and precise representations of it that the Column has preserved for us through the centuries.

Such was the situation at the onset of the Dacian wars – the first (subdivided into three seasonal campaigns) between AD 101 and 102 and the second (subdivided into two campaigns) between 105 and 106 – wars that ended not only in Roman victory but also in the compulsory displacement on a very large scale of the original ethnic components of Dacia, which was afterwards re-populated by Roman colonization. The Roman colonists, mostly veterans or provincials of different provenances, had in the Latin language their only common bond; and this is the main reason why the Thracian dialects, spoken by the original Dacians, are forgotten, whereas the Rumanian neo-Latin island still survives among languages of Slavonic derivation. C. Daicoviciu (1969)*, however, recently re-emphasized his view that the eradication of the original Dacian population

*For this and subsequent references see the Bibliography.

28

by the Romans was not as complete as is usually thought. He bases this belief on solid historical, ethnographical and topographical evidence.

The geographical situation

It is useful at this point to sketch in outline the geographical and strategic situation of the Dacian wars. Only the sites pertinent to the Trajanic campaigns will be quoted here, in particular the Roman bases in Pannonia and Moesia, the parts of the Danube crossed by the Roman army corps, and the probable course of the Roman march of conquest into Dacian territory. The related problems of topography and toponymy are mostly based upon a comparison of modern maps with a Roman one, Peutinger's 9 Table, which will be examined in greater detail later.

In the Roman province of Pannonia our interest is centred *Fig. i* upon the military strongpoints of Siscia (Sisak) and Sirmium (Mitrovica), both situated on the important river-way of the Savus (Sava), that runs from west to east through Yugoslavia. At the confluence of the Savus and the Danube lay Singidunum (near Belgrade). South of this place, following the right bank of the Danube, one entered the province of Moesia Superior and *Fig. ii* reached the stronghold of Viminacium (Kostolaz), not far from the confluence of the Danube and the Margus (Morava). Downstream, beyond Viminacium, the Danube narrows into the gorges of the Iron Gates (of Orsova), where the violent spate of the stream made navigation practically impossible in Roman times. At the Gates' exit, near Drobetae (Turnu Severin), the river broadens anew, navigation becomes easy, the river-banks flatten down and, on the Roman side, there were the ports of Ratiaria, Oescus and Novae (Svishtov), the last two in Moesia Inferior (Bulgaria).

As key points for launching operations into Dacia the fort- *Fig. iii* resses of Viminacium and Pontes (Kladovo) were chosen. Viminacium, upstream from the Iron Gates (of Orsova) and close to the right bank, was also reached by the waterway of the Savus and by the military road of the Dravus (Drava) valley from the west and north, and by that of the Margus valley from the south. Pontes, beyond the Gates, was easily approached from the Black Sea by barges going upstream along the wide lower course of the Danube, and by land through the open plains of Lower Moesia.

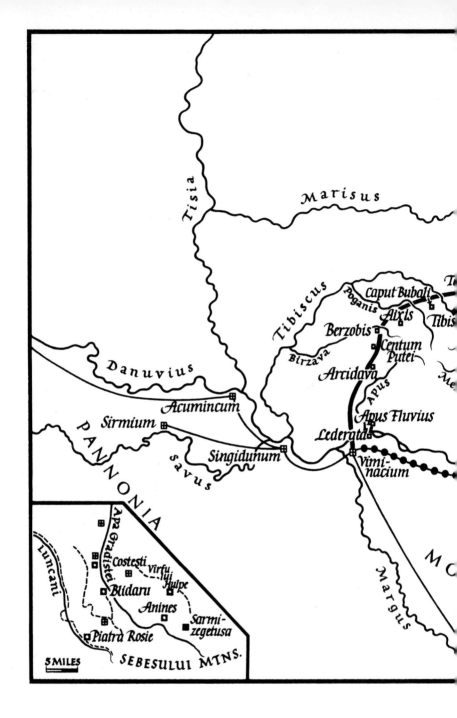

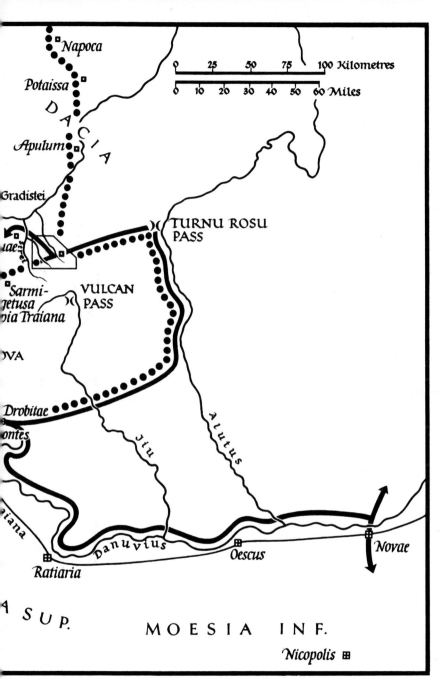

Fig. iii Routes and manoeuvres of the Roman army during the two Dacian wars. The unbroken line indicates the First, and the dotted line the Second Dacian War.

Hence Trajan threw the great bridges of boats across the Danube at Pontes and near Viminacium (at Lederata), the former destined to be replaced by a permanent structure designed by Apollodorus. In order to make the vital communication between these two main bases as sure and rapid as possible through the gorge of the Iron Gates, twelve miles of road were cut, as has been said, in the rock of the bank and widened by cantilevered planks. An inscription carved in the rock itself (*Tabula Traiana*) still commemorates this 'cyclopean' work, the remnants of which have recently been submerged by an artificial reservoir (see p. 49).*

Once the crossing of the Danube was adequately established, the Roman army had to march on towards the Dacian capital, Sarmizegetusa, which is situated in a hilly district, accessible from the west through the Bistra valley by the so-called Iron Gates of Transylvania (not to be confused with those of the Danube), across which a fortified barrage was laid at Tapae. In addition, from the north and south the town was covered by a system of forts, which will be considered below.

It must be borne in mind first of all that the Dacian capital was not at the site recorded on modern maps, which mark the Roman colony *Ulpia Traiana Sarmizegetusa*, but twenty-five miles north-east in the heart of the Sebesului Mountains at
Fig. ii Gradistea Muncelului (Transylvanian Alps). Following the local network of original Dacian tracks we can see that there
Figs. ii, iii were not many approaches to Sarmizegetusa from the north, apart from the one along the Apa Gradistei valley. There is also a surviving stretch of road from the north-west. The most suitable routes would have been those from the west, converging on the high valley of Luncani (probably connected with the Bistra or the Mehadia valley) and from the south-east from the Vulcan and Turnu Rosu passes. As a matter of fact, remains of Roman

*P. Petrovic (Communic. viii, Instit. pour la Protection des Monuments historiques de la Rep. Soc. de Serbie, Belgrade, 1969, pp. 51–53) draws attention to the remains, near Sip, of a navigable canal and the discovery at Karatas of an inscription, dated AD 101, which proclaims that Trajan 'because of the danger of cataracts diverted the river and made navigation on the Danube safe.' The construction of this canal, which coincides in part with the direction of the modern canal of Sip, is very close in date and topography to Trajan's road-works alongside the Iron Gates; it must have formed part of his massive preparations in this area before his offensive in Dacia.

castra, very probably established in Trajan's times, have been found distributed along the Apa Gradistei and on a line south of Sarmizegetusa. It seems probable, therefore, that the Roman army converged on the Dacian capital from the west (the Teregova pass and Bistra valley), the north (Apa Gradistei) and the south-east (Vulcan or Turnu Rosu pass). *Fig. iii*

In their turn the Dacians had long since provided cover for their capital by fortifying a number of hilltops and turning them into a belt of formidable strongholds (see Appendix B for *58–64* these). Thus the heart of Dacia, centred at Sarmizegetusa itself, was composed of what tradition refers to as the 'fortified hills', where the Dacians assembled to resist and challenge the military power of Rome. All this is shown, with remarkable clarity, on the Column's reliefs.

To control the Apa Gradistei route there were fortresses at Costesti, Blidaru and Anines-Vîrfu lui Hulpe. To block the southern and western approaches a great citadel was built and reinforced at Piatra Rosie (see below). Close to the remains of these Dacian *cetati* forts, the *castra* of the Roman attackers are to be seen. Regularly spaced Roman camps have also been found at strategic spots along an east-west line south of the Dacian hill-stronghold, as a part of a wide *circumvallatio* round the besieged *corona montium*.

Further north, beyond the line of the river Marisus (Mures), there were other important Dacian towns, such as Napoca (Cluj), Potaissa (Turda), and Apulum (Alba Iulia). These centres, however, fell quite easily into Roman hands after the strongest Dacian defences, in the aforementioned fortified enclosure at Tapae, at Sarmizegetusa and in the surrounding hill-forts, were broken down. To approach and attack Sarmizegetusa Trajan was faced with the following alternative routes: a *Fig. iii* direct advance towards the entry of the Bistra valley (Transylvanian Iron Gates), marching through the Banat either from the south-west (Berzovia-Tibiscum) or from the south (Mehadia valley); or an indirect detour for encircling the enemy's position, first marching south-east across the Valachian plain, then turning north up either the Jiu or Olt (Alutus) valleys crossing the passes of Vulcan or of Turnu Rosu respectively, and finally attacking from the east the fortified belt of Sarmizegetusa. An approach from the south could be achieved by both routes.

As will be seen later, the Roman army carried out combined manoeuvres, converging upon its targets from different directions. Peutinger's Table, as well as archaeological discoveries, have afforded some corroboration of the foregoing hypotheses about the routes of the Roman conquest of Dacia, the historical documentation of which is entirely lost.

The First Dacian War began with the crossing of the Danube by means of two great bridges of boats, one between Lederata and Apus Fluvius (Carasul) and the other between Pontes and Drobetae. The Roman army, divided into two main corps, penetrated the Dacian territory up- and downstream of the Danube's Iron Gates. Trajan, in the only surviving words of his diary, stated that the route of the army corps under his own command (clearly represented on the Column) was towards Tibiscum (Caransebes), crossing the rivers Apus (Carasul), Poganis and Birzava, up to Tapae, at the fortified entrance to the Bistra valley. Here the emperor was joined by the other Roman corps, which came by the southern road along the Mehadia (ad Mediam) valley and across the Teregova pass. Thus the blockade of Sarmizegetusa from the west was assured, even if the attempt of the reunited Roman army to break through the Dacian belt in the Transylvanian Alps was unsuccessful. Trajan and part of his army were now probably summoned to a place much farther to the south, in or near Lower Moesia, in order to face and win a struggle against a migrating wave of barbarians, allied to the Dacians.

Fig. iii

The next year, another Roman army crossed the bridge (still of boats) at Drobetae to defile south at the foot of the mountains and then turn north up the Olt valley. Beyond the Turnu Rosu pass the Romans attacked, and eventually overcame, the hill-forts defending Sarmizegetusa from the south-west and north-west. Thus the First Dacian War ended with the surrender of Sarmizegetusa and with Decebalus asking Trajan for mercy and truce in the presence of the Roman army, probably at Aquae (Calan), as the Column suggests. Among the conditions for an armistice was the dismantling of the hill-forts and the evacuation of the entire mountain stronghold. As the Column hints, this was not carried out by the Dacians.

The second war had, as recorded on the Column, a long prelude, with Trajan, escorted by a bodyguard, travelling by sea and land from Ancona to Drobetae, with halts at some

34

harbours of the Adriatic or Aegean Sea (Salonae, Corinth), and with the foundation of Nicopolis. After having reached what was probably Sirmium, Trajan seems to have been summoned in haste to Drobetae by the beginning of the heavy Dacian attack upon the Roman bridgehead which opened the second war. At the head of a body of cavalry, riding fast along the rock-cut road of the Danubian gorge, the emperor arrives at the crucial moment to relieve the Romans' dangerous situation; and in front of his reunited troops he celebrates the consecration of the newly built permanent bridge between Pontes and Drobetae. Then the Roman army crosses this bridge and divides again into two main bodies converging upon Sarmizegetusa, one coming from the east, the other from the west. The Dacian capital is now besieged and assailed from both sides, and the Romans break through the battered walls, in spite of the desperate defence of the Dacians, some of whom escape capture after setting fire to part of the town. The Romans camp inside the conquered city, while auxiliary forces pursue and annihilate the surviving Dacians, cross the Marisus, and capture the centres of northern Dacia, as far as the territory of the Roxolani.

Peutinger's Table and the topography of the Dacian wars

We will now look at the geographical situation in the way a Roman soldier and commander would have done, briefly examining Peutinger's Table, in so far as it concerns the Dacian war-theatre. An officer named Balbus seems to have been in charge of the topographical service in the Dacian wars (Homo, p. 206).

The making of illustrated maps *(itineraria picta)* and the composing of itineraries *(itineraria)*, for both military and civilian purposes, were highly developed arts in Roman times. No doubt the troop-movements and the plan of campaign were carefully outlined by the army staff on geographical and topographical maps, just as they are today (see Vegetius, III, 6). Moreover, it is fairly certain that the transfer of small units, and even of single troopers, was also made on the basis of an officially approved *itinerarium* (St Ambrose, *Comment. ad Psalm. cxviii*, 2). The ordinary soldiers, too, would have been taught some basic geography and they could become interested enough in it to record their own *itinera* (travels) through the empire, as

9

9 Peutinger's Table, segments vi and vii. A typical Roman road-map.

Fig. iv Sketch of the scroll partially unwound showing continental Europe and North Africa. The rectangles indicate the Dacian war theatre.

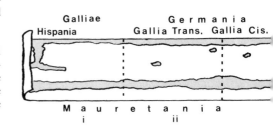

one man did on a map painted on a shield found at Dura Europos on the Euphrates.

From the civilian standpoint, map-making was of equal importance both for private trade and for the government post-service, the *cursus publicus*, which was an efficient world-wide organization for the transmission of official correspondence and goods and for the transport of civil and military officials when on duty.

The main documents of Roman *itineraria* which we possess are the painted *Tabula* and the written *Itinerarium Antonini*, both covering the whole empire and some territories beyond it.

36

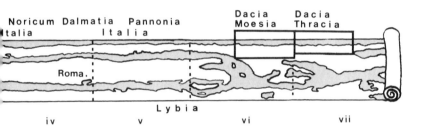

Peutinger's Table has been chosen here to recreate some 'feeling' of Roman military topography, inasmuch as it is a 'real' map in the modern sense. The original was probably a drawing made under the Late Empire, itself derived from an early-imperial (Augustan) official model; this was probably the monumental map of Agrippa, engraved on marble and set up under the Porticus Octaviae in Rome. Its display on a long wall could have had some bearing on the special form of the map itself (see below). What we have is a copy of a lost original map made by a monk of Colmar in AD 1265 and acquired in 1508 by a soldier named Peutinger.

37

Leaving aside the many arguments that have arisen over the cosmography and cartography of antiquity, which are a matter for a more specialized study, we may say that the Table does not fulfil the current Ptolemaic criteria as regards projection and scale, but was rather designed to satisfy practical requirements; it thus reflects the realistic mentality of the Romans.

The map is a long band made up of eleven (originally twelve: the first, Britannia, is lost) rectangular segments of parchment measuring altogether over eight yards in length and only one and a half feet in height. Thus it just fits into a *volumen*, the normal scroll of the Romans, and was easy to read, handy to consult (by simultaneously unrolling and re-rolling the two ends), and of a standard size for transport.

In an *à vol d'oiseau* view southern and central Europe, North Africa and the Middle East are deployed on the band, an arrangement that could not but result in gross distortion. Rome, for instance, faces Carthage. Nevertheless, if one considers that the seas are reduced in size, since they have no purpose in a non-nautical map such as this one, and that a fairly good orientation west–east is maintained, the general outline of the sub-continents is easily recognizable. Designed as a road map *(itinerarium)*, the Table provides a fine display of the imperial road-networks, on which the distances, quite out of scale, are carefully indicated in between each place. Each tract of road is artificially indented in order to make room for the mile-numbering (leagues in Gallia, parasangs in Persia) and town-names. Mountains, rivers, and harbours are sketchily drawn, and the main halting-places are marked by differently conventionalized buildings, in a way which probably followed the official symbolism used for the *cursus publicus* (Levi and Levi). Thus the twin turret would indicate a *hospitium* (a simple hostel), a gabled-roof house a *mansio* (a tavern), a temple-like building a *mutatio* for changing mounts, a square building with a water basin in the centre a *statio* (a well-equipped hotel with public bath), often at places named *Aquae*, a long building a *horreum* (corn-depot). Big towns are personified or shown with walls and major buildings.

Some of these type-symbols may well have been adopted for the representation of buildings in the background of the Column's frieze, just as they were in the much later *Notitia Dignitatum*.

The map was probably coloured in tints signifying localities: seas and rivers green, water of baths at *stationes* light blue, for example, with a yellowish background for plains and red or grey for mountains. Owing to the extended west–east distortion of the Roman empire, and to the special importance attributed to the countries therein, southern Europe receives more than its share of space in the band's central strip, while the peripheral provinces and territories are squeezed alongside the map's margins. Dacia is, then, confined to the upper edge of the sixth and seventh segments, together with the nearby Danubian provinces. The actual war-theatre is in the sixth segment. But in spite of the arbitrary distortions in the layout, this kind of map served very well anybody who intended to travel and campaign in the Roman world; and it was therefore very probably employed in the Dacian wars. The topographical links that have long been suggested between the places and routes of the Table and of the Column support this view. One should bear in mind, however, that Peutinger's Table, using a late imperial *itinerarium*, represents a Roman world somewhat different from that of Trajan's time. For instance, the Sarmategte (Sarmizegetusa) represented fourteen miles from Ad Aquas *(segment vi)* must be *Colonia Ulpia Traiana Sarmizegetusa* and not the original Dacian capital with which we are concerned, situated about twenty-five miles away (see pp. 223–24).

10 The captive Dacian, a noble wearing a cap, possibly Decebalus, symbolizes *Dacia capta*, the defeated Dacia, sitting on a shield in a mourning attitude; below lies the national weapon, the battle-scythe. *Denarius* of Trajan, M. & S. 216.

CHAPTER II

THE IMPACT MADE BY TRAJAN'S ACHIEVEMENTS IN DACIA

Official commemoration and popular tradition

The enormous effect of Trajan's achievements in Dacia from the psychological viewpoint can be gauged by their commemoration within the Roman world and by the echoes of them that resounded far beyond its geographical and chronological limits.

First of all, we can sense even today the impact made by Trajan's Dacian wars throughout the empire by glancing at examples of the coinage relating to them. This exhibits an extremely rich and varied number of reverse-types emphasizing the victory of Rome, the triumph of Trajan, the humiliation of the foe and the expansion of the empire.

Furthermore, there is a fairly rich body of epigraphical material dealing with the Dacian wars. Though this is a subject for specialized study, it may be useful to include here some extracts from inscriptions, with translations, which have a bearing on the army represented on the Column (Romano-British inscriptions, in particular).

Finally, it is of particular value to make a careful examination of the complex of commemorative monuments found not so very far from the main battlefield, namely those at Tropaeum Traiani (the modern Adamklissi) in the province of Moesia Inferior. These comprise, in close proximity to one another, the ruins of an altar (a cenotaph), a mausoleum, and a huge triumphal monument, the Tropaeum Traiani, adorned with a series of sculptured 'metopes' representing scenes of war 22–5 against the Dacians. This monument is of outstanding importance for studying provincial commemorative art and, even more, for tracing the lost history of the Dacian wars and restoring them to life through the evidence of pictures. Indeed, one could describe the Trophy as the provincial counterpart of the Column in Rome. By comparing the two series of pictures we can appreciate the events' imperial significance (from the Roman monument), and, at the same time, what they meant to the soldiers on the spot (from the Adamklissi monument). But first let us note how far in space and time Trajan's fame travelled in popular tradition, from Antiquity into the Middle Ages.

From the eastern plains of Ukraina the gallant Sarmato-Scythian allies of the Dacians had come to fight Rome, and back they went to their distant, frosty steppes after experiencing the weight of defeat and the impact of Roman might. Trajan, the invincible conqueror from the West, thus became a mythical, divine hero, entering the pantheon of the peoples who eventually evolved into proto-Russian Slavs. One thousand years later, the name of Trajan is still mentioned in awe, in the *chanson de gestes* of Igor's legion (IX, 57: 'Once, Trajan's slaughters had been . . .').

In the Christian West, where the memory of the pagan Roman emperors was so often execrated, that of Trajan was unique in being praised and honoured. The legend grew up that Pope Gregory the Great, confronted with the Column and touched by the thought of Trajan's virtues, prayed for and obtained the salvation of his soul. Then, in Dante's Paradise, Trajan shines high up in the ethereal eagle's glory: he is indeed

> *dei cinque che mi fan cerchio per ciglio*
> *colui che più al becco mi s'accosta*

('among the five who encircle my eyelash, the one who is the closest to my beak'), up in the sixth sky (*Paradiso*, XX, 31–48).

The Dacian wars on Roman coinage

After the end of the First Dacian War a series of reverse-types were struck which allude directly to Trajan's victories. These coins are dated between AD 102 and 114, spanning the emperor's fourth, fifth and sixth consulships, and the obverses frequently include in their legends the title of *Dacicus*, bestowed on the emperor either late in 102 or early in 103. It is often

11 Dacia kneeling before *Pax*. *Denarius* of Trajan, BMC 216.

12 Dacia before Rome, who has a spear and a statuette of Victory on her outstretched arm. *Sestertius* of Trajan, M. & S. 534.

impossible to link these coins definitely with one or other of the wars. But we can observe in them a variety of trends in the official method of commemoration.

A 'realistic' trend would seem to be represented on reverses relating to actual events and bearing a special significance easily understood by the spectator. Into this series fall the scenes in which a Dacian captive appears alone, either standing with hands bound or kneeling or seated in an attitude of despair on his shield and weapons, all reproduced in precise detail (e.g. the cap and the curved *falx*). Elsewhere, the motif of *Dacia capta* is associated either with the figure of the emperor or with the personification of Rome and such traditional Roman figures as the Senate, the Tiber, or *Pax Romana*, so as to create a complex of a semi-realistic kind with a more emphatic commemorative significance. Thus we have the Dacian (Decebalus?) presenting his shield to Trajan, the captive presented by Trajan himself to the Senate, the captive kneeling in front of Rome or *Pax*, the figure of the Tiber with his knee on *Dacia* whom he forces on the ground, and the Dacian's head under the foot of the standing emperor. The representation of Dacians captured and humiliated by the Romans, in the presence of Trajan, is quite common both on the Column and on the Adamklissi monument.

10, 15–16

11, 12

43

13 The classic triumphal image of the Emperor on horseback, thrusting his spear at a falling enemy (a Dacian) while galloping over him. *Sestertius* of Trajan, M. & S. 534.

Of special impact, and intermediate between actuality and allegory in imperial commemoration, is the classic picture of
13 Trajan on horseback, thrusting his spear at a fallen Dacian. It is worth recalling that this epic scene, charged with symbolic implications that go beyond its merely martial character, had been widely used in imperial figurative art; and that coins with reverse-types showing this motif were struck, it seems, in great quantities. On the other hand, this scene is absent on the Column, and can only be recognized with uncertainty on one 'metope' of the Adamklissi Tropaeum. Another typical rendering in realistic terms of Roman victory and triumph is that of the emperor riding in a *quadriga* and holding either the eagle-topped sceptre or the laurel branch.

Among the above motifs, that of *Dacia capta*, defeated and humiliated, belongs partly to the realm of more abstract representation, typified by the 'pile of arms' *(congeries armorum)* and by the trophy itself. Very common are the reverses with *Dacia* seated in a mourning attitude upon a pile of shields, curved swords and long spears, or beside a trophy. Common,

44

14 The Emperor crowned by Victory. *Sestertius* of Trajan, BMC 825.

15 A Dacian seated in grief on a pile of arms and shields; scythes are visible on the left. *Denarius* of Trajan, BMC 391.

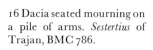

16 Dacia seated mourning on a pile of arms. *Sestertius* of Trajan, BMC 786.

17, 18 A typical Dacian trophy on the reverse of a *denarius* of Trajan, BMC 391. It is identical with that reproduced on the column at the left of the Victory (18) who separates the two wars.

19 The personification of Victory, inscribing *Victoria Dacia* on her shield. Trajanic *denarius*, BMC 322.

20 The rendering of the Column engraved on a Trajanic *denarius* (BMC 454) is very realistic, but it overemphasizes the statue at the top.

too, are the types with *Dacia* supporting a trophy on her shoulders, or crushed beneath the foot of Trajan, who is erecting a trophy.

The purely symbolic trend is represented by the type of the simple 'Dacian trophy', with the usual elements of central 17 cuirass or tunic, casque at the top, and lateral shields, erected on crossed poles, at the base of which there is often the pile of arms, sometimes including specifically Dacian weapons. The figure of the emperor or that of Mars may be associated with this trophy. Trophies of this kind are also represented on the Column, while this self-same trophy is the *episema* at the top of the Adamklissi monument. Moreover, both the Column itself 20 and the Tropaeum Traiani appear as coin reverse-types from Roman and provincial mints respectively.

To the same symbolic trend belongs the classical personification of winged Victory, either inscribing DA CI CA or VIC 19 DAC on an oval shield or adorning a trophy or crowning the emperor. The first type is that represented on the Column, but 14 without words on the shield, at the centre of the spirals, serving 18 to separate the two wars. The shield alone, with the inscription DACIA CAPTA, is the simplest way of commemorating the victory.

However, in the Roman concept of victory, the major aim was not to defeat and humiliate the enemy but rather to draw him into the orbit of romanization through that imposition of *pax* on the civilian population (cf. the Virgilian '. . . pacisque imponere morem') which normally followed in the footsteps of

47

21 The reverse of Trajan's *sestertius* with the legend *Dacia Augusta Provincia* (BMC 960) symbolized and celebrated the Roman's military colonization of subdued Dacia.

the actual conquest of the territory. Hence we find that the romanization of the new province of Dacia is commemorated both on the coinage and on the Column. Between AD 112 and 114 the reverse-type, with the legend DACIA AVGVST 21 PROVINCIA, was struck: the personification of the province is seated peacefully and holding proudly a legionary standard, while children, with corn and grapes, play on her lap. The correct interpretation of this allegory has been supplied by Professor J. M. C. Toynbee, who states that it links together the 'military' (the standard) and 'colony' (children and harvest) symbols as a clear allusion to the colonization of Dacia by army veterans. This is in perfect accord both with history and, in the 156 sphere of art, with one of the final scenes on the Column, where a group of short-cloaked, bearded men, all *in caliga* (i.e. wearing the sandals peculiar to the Roman soldier), is in the act of marching into the land evacuated by the natives. They are, indeed, Trajan's veterans, who will re-populate and romanize Dacia for the centuries to come.

48

Inscriptions relating to the Dacian wars

The dedicatory inscription on the base of Trajan's Column (Smallwood, 378, p. 128):

SENATVS POPVLVSQVE ROMANVS / IMP. CAESARI DIVI NERVAE
F. NERVAE / TRAIANO AVG. GERM.DACICO PONTIF. / MAXIMO
TRIB.POT. XVII IMP.VI COS.VI P.P. / AD DECLARANDVM
QVANTAE ALTITVDINIS / MONS ET LOCVS TANT [is oper]
IBVS SIT EGESTVS

The Senate and the people of Rome to the Emperor Caesar, son of the divine Nerva, Nerva Trajan Augustus Germanicus Dacicus, *pontifex maximus*, at the time of his seventeenth tribunician power, of his sixth imperial salutation, and of his sixth consulship, the Father of the Country, to declare how high a hill and place have been excavated for these great works.

Inscription cut in the cliff-face on the right bank of the Danube west of Orsova (Smallwood, 413, p. 135; *ILS* 5863):

IMP. CAESAR DIVI NERVAE F. NERVA TRAIANVS AVG.GERM.
PONTIF. MAXIMVS TRIB.POT.IIII PATER PATRIAE COS.III
MONTIBUS EXCISI[S] ANCO[ni]BUS SUBLAT[i]S VIA[m] F[ecit]

The Emperor Caesar, son of the divine Nerva, Nerva Trajan Augustus Germanicus, *pontifex maximus*, at the time of his fourth tribunician power, the Father of the Country, at the time of his third consulate, after cutting down mountains and removing their projecting elbows, made the road.

The dedicatory inscription of the great Trophy at Adam-klissi (Smallwood, 303, p. 104; Picard, p. 394):

MA[rti] VLTORI / IMP. [Caes] AR DIVI / NERVA[e] [f.] NERVA
[Tr] AIANVS AV [g.] [Germ.] / [Dac] I [cus] P [on] T. MA
[x.] / [trib.] [potes] T. XIII / [imp.] VI [cos.] V P. P. / . . .
[Smallwood's version goes on] [per exerc?] ITV [m. . .]
SV. . . E. . . [Picard's version] [et] [exerc] ITV[s] [Moesiae] /
[inferioris] SV [b]

To Mars the Avenger, the Emperor Caesar, son of the divine Nerva, Nerva Trajan Augustus Germanicus

Dacicus, *pontifex maximus*, at the time of his thirteenth tribunician power, of his sixth imperial salutation, and of the fifth consulate, the Father of the Country . . . [Picard's version] the army of Lower Moesia. . .

The dedicatory inscription of the cenotaph, the Dacian war memorial, at Adamklissi (*ILS* 9107):

. . .[Trajan, etc.] [Tri] B.POT. . .[in] MEMORIAM FORTISS [imorum] [virorum] [qui] PRO REP. MORTE OCCVB[uerunt] [c]OL. NEAPOL.ITAL. PRAE[f] . . . [several names]

Trajan . . . tribunician power . . . In memory of the bravest of men who met death for the commonwealth . . . Prefect, from the *colonia* of Naples, in Italy . . .

MILITARY DIPLOMAS* recording auxiliary soldiers and units that took part in the Dacian wars:

A crack unit from Britain is granted the Roman citizenship, and other honorific titles, for outstanding service in Dacia. Trajan to Novantico, 11 August, AD 106 (a double bronze tablet found at Porolissum; *CIL* XVI, Suppl. 160):

IMP. CAESAR DIVI NERVAE F.NERVA TRAIA / NVS AVGVSTVS GERMANIC.DACICVS / PONTIF.MAXIMVS TRIBVN.POTEST. / XIIII IMP.VI COS.V P.P. / PEDITBVS ET EQVITIBVS QVI MILI- TANT / IN COHORTE I BRITTONVM MILLIARIA / VLPIA TORQVATA P.F.CIVIVM ROMA / NORVM QVAE ESTIN DACIA SVB D. / TERENTIO SCAVRIANO QUORVM NO / MINA SVB SCRIPTA SVNT PIE ET FIDELI / TER EXPEDITIONE DACICA FVNCTIS / ANTE EMERITA STIPENDIA CIVITA / TEM ROMANAM DEDIT / A.D.III IDVS AVG. / DARNITHITI / L.MINICIO NATALE / Q.SILVANO GRANIANO COS. / PEDITI / M. VLPIO ADCOBROVATI F.NOVANTICO / NI / RATIS / .DESCRIPTVM ET RECOGNITVM EX TA / BVLA AENEA QVAE FIXA EST RO / MAE IN MVRO. POST TEMPLVM / DIVI AVG.AD MINERVAM

The Emperor Caesar, son of the divine Nerva, Nerva Trajan Augustus Germanicus Dacicus, *pontifex maximus*,

---

*It may be of help to readers of Roman military inscriptions to know that the symbol ∞ means *milliaria* (for a cohort), while the signs > or Ɔ stand for *centuria* or *centurion*.

at the time of his fourteenth tribunician power, of his sixth imperial salutation and fifth consulate, the Father of the Country, to the horse- and foot-soldiers serving with the first cohort of Britons, 1000 men strong, Ulpia, decorated with the collar of honour, obedient and faithful, of Roman citizens, which is in Dacia under D. Terentius Scaurianus, and whose names are written below, who served with obedience and loyalty in the Dacian expedition, before the completion of their terms of service [thereby] granted the Roman citizenship. 11 August, at Darnithitis, the consuls being L. Minicius Natalis and Q. Silvanus Granianus. To the infantryman M. Ulpius, Adcobrovatus' son, Novantico, from Ratae (Coritanorum–Leicester). Copied from and compared with the bronze tablet fixed, at Rome, to the wall behind the temple of divine Augustus, near Minerva's temple.

On the other tablet, the names of the witnesses are listed:

P.CORNELI ALEXANDRI / L.PVLLI VERECVNDI / P.ATINI AMERIMNI / C.TVTICANI SATVRNINI / L.PVLLI TROPHIMI / C.IVLI PARATI / M.IVNI EVTYCHI

A similar diploma, found in Hungary. Trajan to Thaemus, 17 February, AD 110 (*CIL* XVI, Suppl. 57):

IMP.CAESAR DIVI NERVAE F.NERVA TRAIA / NVS AVG.GERM. DACICVS PONTIF.MAXIMVS / TRIBVNIC.POTESTAT. XIIII IMP.VI COS. V P.P. / EQVITIBVS ET PEDITIBVS QVI MILITAVERVNT IN / ALIS DVABVS ET COHORTIBVS DECEM QVAE AP / PELLANTVR I CIVIVM ROMANORVM ET I AVG. / ITVRAEORVM ET I AVG. ITVRAEORVM SAGIT / TAR.ET I BRITANNICA ∞ C.R.ET I HISPANOR. / P.F.ET I THRACVM C.R.ET I ITVRAEORVM ET I / FLAVIA VLPIA HISPANORVM ∞ C.R.ET II GAL / LORVM MACEDONICA ET III CAMPESTRIS C.R. / ET IIII CYPRIA C.R.ET VIII RAETORVM C.R. / ET PEDITES SINGVLARES BRITANNICI ET SVNT / IN DACIA SVB D.TERENTIO SCAVRIANO QVINIS / ET VICENIS PLVRIBVSVE STIPENDIIS EMERITIS / DIMISSIS HONESTA MISSIONE QVORVM NO / MINA SVBSCRIPTA SVNT IPSIS LIBERIS POSTE / RISQVE EORVM CIVITATEM DEDIT ET CONV / BIVM CVM VXORIBVS QVAS TVNC HABVISSENT / CVM EST CIVITAS IIS DATA AVT SI QVI CAELI/BES ESSENT CVM IIS

QVAS POSTEA DVXISSENT / DVMTAXAT SINGVLI SINGVLAS.A.D.
XIII K.MART. / SER.SCIPIONE SALVIDIENO ORFITO / M. PEDV-
CAEO PRISCINO COS. / ALAE. I AVG.ITVRAEOR. CVI PRAEST /
C.VETTIVS PRISCVS / EX GREGALE / THAEMO HORATI F.
ITVRAEO / ET NAL. F.EIVS ET MARCO F.EIVS ET ANTONIO F.
EIVS / .DESCRIPTVM ET RECOGNITVM EX TABVLA / AENEA
QVAE FIXA EST ROMAE IN MVRO POST / TEMPLVM DIVI AVG.AD
MINERVAM

The Emperor Caesar [titles as above] to the horse- and
foot soldiers who served with two *alae* and ten cohorts, the
names of which are: 1st of Roman citizens and 1st
Augusta of Ituraeans and 1st of Ituraean archers and 1st
of Britons – 1000 men strong – Roman citizens and 1st of
Spaniards – obedient and faithful – and 1st of Thracians,
Roman citizens, and 1st of Ituraeans and 1st of Spaniards
Flavia Ulpia – 1000 men strong – of Roman citizens and
2nd of Gauls Macedonica and 3rd of Yeomanry, Roman
citizens, and 4th of Cypriots, Roman citizens, and 8th of
Raeti, Roman citizens, and selected British infantrymen,
also being in Dacia under D. Terentius Scaurianus, who
have fulfilled their twenty-five – or more – years of service
and are honourably discharged from the army, whose
names are written below, to themselves and to their sons
and descendants is granted the Roman citizenship and
the status of legal marriage with the wives that they had at
the time the citizenship was granted; or for those who
were bachelors the right of legal marriage with the brides
to whom they will afterwards get married, provided that
each man has only one wife. 17 February, the consuls
being Ser. Scipio Salvidienus Orfitus and M. Peduceus
Priscinus: to the ex-private in the ala Augusta of Ituraeans
– commanded by C. Vettius Priscus – Thaemus, Horace's
son, Ituraean, and to his sons Nalius[?], Marcus and
Antonius. Copied from, and compared with . . . [as above].

The service of a future emperor in the Dacian campaign (an
inscription at Athens; *CIL* III,550):

. . .AELIO. . .SERG.HADRIANO / . . .[some civilian titles]
IMP.NERVAE TRAIANI / CAESARIS AVG.GERMANICI DACICI
PANNONIAE INFERIORIS PRAETORI EODEMQVE / TEMPORE

LEG.LEG.I MINERVIAE P.F.BELLO. DACICO ITEM TRIB.PLEB. QVAESTORI IMPERATORIS / TRAIANI ET COMITI EXPEDITIONIS DACICAE DONIS MILITARIBVS AB EO DONATO. . .[etc.] [other titles follow]

To Aelius Sergius Hadrian . . . of the Emperor Nerva Trajan Caesar Augustus Germanicus Dacicus, *praetor* of Pannonia Inferior and, at this time, *legatus* [commander] of the 1st Minervian legion, obedient and faithful, in the Dacian war and also *tribunus plebis* and *quaestor* of the Emperor Trajan and his companion [adviser] in the Dacian expedition, having from him received military decorations...

The many decorations (see p. 79) earned by a gallant officer, eventually to become a consul, in the Dacian campaign (an inscription at Turin; *CIL* V, 6977):

. . .[Glitio]. . .[Stel.Atilio]. . .AGRICOLAE COS.II / . . . [civilian titles] LEGAT.PRO PR. / IMP.NERVAE.CAES.TRAIAN. AVG.GER.DACICI / PROVINC.PANNON.DONATO AB EODEM / BELLO DACICO DONIS MILITARIBVS CORONA / MVRALI VAL-LARI CLASSIC.AVREA HAST. / PVRIS IIII VEXILLIS IIII LEGATO PRO PR. / PROVINC.BELGIC.DIVI NERVAE LEG. / LEG.VI FERRAT . . . [etc.] [other command posts]

. . . To . . . Glitius Atilius Agricola, twice a consul . . . *legatus propraetore* of the Emperor Nerva Caesar Trajan Augustus Germanicus Dacicus in the province of Pan-nonia, from him having received the military decorations of the crown for gallant wall-assault, that for gallant ditch-assault, that for gallant naval [or, better, amphibious] operations, that of gold, four spear-heads of pure [silver], four banners, *legatus propraetore* in the province of Belgica and divine Nerva's *legatus* [commander] of the 6th legion Ferrata ['Ironsides']...

Another gallant officer, decorated in the Dacian campaign, who held posts of command in auxiliary and legionary units (an inscription at Contigliano, near Reate; *CIL* IX,4753):

PRIFERNIO. . .PAETO / MEMMIO APOLLINARI / . . .[civilian titles] / PRAEF.COH. III BREVC. TRIB.LEG. X / GEM.PRAEF.

ALAE.I ASTVRVM DONIS / DONATO EXPED.DAC.AB IMP. /
TRAIANO HASTA PVRA VEXILLO / CORONA MVRALI. . .
[civilian titles follow]

To Prifernius Paetus Memmius Apollinaris . . . prefect of
the 3rd cohort of Breuci, tribune of the 10th 'twin' legion
(Gemina), prefect of the 1st *ala* of Asturians, who received in the Dacian expedition from the Emperor
Trajan the military decorations of the spearhead of pure
silver, of the banner, and of the crown for gallant wall-
assault . . .

The brilliant career of an officer, which began with the command of a unit of 'irregulars' in the Dacian war (an inscription
at Ujo, near Oviedo; Smallwood, 301, p. 102):

C.SVLPIC.VRSVLO PRAEF.SYMMACHIARIORVM ASTVRVM BELLI
DACICI ƆLEG.I MINERVIAE P.F. Ɔ COH.XII VRBANAE Ɔ COH.IIII
PRAETORIAE P.P.LEG.XIIX PR.ET LEG.III AVG. . .[the dedica-
tor's name]

To C. Sulpicius Ursulus, prefect of the 'irregular unit'
[*symmachiarii*] of Asturians in the Dacian war, centurion of
the 1st Minervian legion, obedient and faithful, centurion
of the 12th urban cohort, centurion of the 4th praetorian
cohort, *primus pilus* of the 22nd [?] legion [Primigenia ?]
and of the 3rd Augustan legion . . .

A legionary of British origin who served with the 30th
legion Ulpia Victrix (an inscription from Xanten; *CIL* XIII,
8631):

MATRIBVS / BRITTIS / S.VALERIVS / SIMPLEX / MIL.LEG.XXX /
V.V. / V.S.L.M.

To the British Mothers, S. Valerius Simplex, a soldier of
the 30th legion Ulpia Victrix, gladly and duly fulfils his
vow.

A British auxiliary unit is likely to have taken part in com-
pany with other units in the construction of the great bridge at
Pontes-Drobetae (an inscription found in one of the pillars of
the bridge, at Drobetae; *CIL* III,1703):

COH.II HISP / . . .H I CRE. / [CO] H.III.BRIT.

The 2nd cohort of Spaniards . . . the 1st cohort of Cretans, the 3rd cohort of Britons.

A possible hint at the perilous campaigning along the Olt's valley and in the hilly strongholds of Dacia by a legionary of the 1st Minervian legion (an inscription at Cologne; *CIL* XIII,8213):

MATRONIS / AVFANIB.C. / IVL.MANSVE / TVS M. L. I. M. / P.F. V.S.L.M. FV[I] / T AD ALVTVM / FLVMEN SECVS / MONT. CAVCAS.

To the Aufanian Mothers Julius Mansuetus, a soldier of the 1st Minervian legion, obedient and faithful, gladly and duly fulfils his vow. He was on the river Alutus [Olt] near the Caucasus Mountains.*

The Tropaeum Traiani at Adamklissi

The complex of monuments at Adamklissi (in Dobruja, 40 miles from Constanta) comprises a war memorial, in the form of an altar (a cenotaph), and a mausoleum, about 200 yards apart, and the great Tropaeum Traiani. The cenotaph, badly ruined, was inscribed with a long list of names of fallen Roman service-men, headed by the statement that it is 'in memory of the bravest of men who lost their lives for the Roman commonwealth' in one of the Dacian wars. The list opens with a high-ranking officer [PRAE *(fectus)*] from Naples, whose name is, however, illegible (see p. 50). This name has given rise to much discussion. Some think it impossible that the name could be that of Cornelius Fuscus, who, as we have seen, fell in the Dacian disasters of Domitian's reign, and have surmised (Baradez, p. 209) that it was that of a *praefectus castrorum* of Trajan's time. The names that follow are those of Italian and Roman soldiers (probably praetorians), of junior officers *(signiferi, imaginiferi)*, and of many *auxilia*.

The cenotaph and mausoleum are obviously related in purpose to the major monument, the Trophy, sacred to Mars

Fig. i

---

*It is an open question as to whether the river is the Alontas, which flows from the Caucasus mountains into the Caspian Sea, or whether Alutus is correct and the 'Caucasus' are the Transylvanian Alps.

the Avenger *(Marti Ultori)*. Roman dedications to this god were intended either to obliterate the dishonour of a previous defeat or to record the recovery of military standards lost in a disastrous campaign *(signa recepta)*.

The site of these monuments, at the crossing of the natural routes between Bessarabia (and the East) and southern Europe, marks a position of no small geographical importance in Rome's Balkan provinces.

The Tropaeum is an imposing work for a peripheral province. In fact it recalls the Alpine Trophy of Augustus at La Turbie. It consists of a circular drum 100 feet in diameter and about 50 feet high, encased in masonry, standing upon a round platform with seven steps, and crowned with a conical roof made of large imbricated slabs. At the top rises the Trophy, namely a tree-trunk, on which are hung a cuirass, shields, and spears, with the figures of four prisoners at its foot. It stands on a double hexagonal tower, which bears the dedicatory inscription: '. . . to Mars the Avenger . . . Trajan . . . and the army of Moesia Inferior . . .' (Picard) (see p. 49).

22–5   On the upper part of the drum, fifty-four 'metopes', each measuring about 5×4 feet and adorned with reliefs representing war scenes, were placed in close proximity to one another and bordered above and below by decorative friezes. Above them were twenty-six more panels, spaced along the upper edge of the drum, forming crenellations; each was carved with the figure of a chained prisoner. In the spaces between these panels were lions set against a background of geometric designs. The whole architectural complex, from *crepis* to *episema*, was 100 feet high. Only parts of the drum and of its steps are *in situ* today. Fortunately, thanks to Rumanian archaeologists, all the fragments that had been scattered around or removed, and nearly all the 'metopes', have been carefully re-arranged and preserved in a modern adjacent museum.

The systematic study of this monument, between the end of the last century and the appearance of the recent monograph by F. B. Florescu, has served to indicate the enormous archaeological, historical and ethnographical problems which the Trophy raises.

First of all, the significance of the inscriptions, the subject of the 'metopes' and the date of the entire work have given rise to very divergent theories, which may be summarized as follows:

1. The monument was originally a trophy celebrating the victory of Crassus over the Bastarnae in 28 BC (Furtwängler in Picard, p. 395).

2. It commemorated a success of Trajan over the Roxolani in AD 100 (First Dacian War) and was erected in the very place of the defeat suffered by Oppius Sabinus fifteen years before, during Domitian's Dacian War (Salmon, p. 277).

3. It was a Trajanic work, erected after the two Dacian wars in AD 109 and substantially remade in the fourth century by Constantine, or even later. On one 'metope' Constans II, in place of Trajan, has been recognized (Ferri).

4. It was related to a 'Third Dacian War', when Rome defeated Scythian nomads from the steppes, not true Dacians, in AD 108 – a war unrecorded in history and quite different from the wars depicted on the Roman Column (Richmond, 1967).

5. It celebrated an actual battle that took place at Adamklissi during the First Dacian War and was won by Trajan and his army at a heavy cost (there were thousands of fallen Romans, including a *praefectus castrorum*). This victory saved the fortunes of the campaign from the grave danger of a 'diversion' attack by the Dacians and their allies on the province of Lower Moesia, 200 miles south of the main war-theatre. History has, again, nothing to say about any struggle in Lower Moesia at the time: the evidence of the Column proves that Trajan with some units embarked, landed, fought and re-embarked in the course of the first war, and this episode was long ago interpreted (Petersen) as a Lower Moesian diversion campaign (see below). The connection of the Tropaeum with the avenging of previous Roman disasters was not admitted (Tocilescu, Baradez), in spite of the clear indication given by the dedication *Marti Ultori*.

The author shares the opinion of those who believe the Tropaeum to be a Trajanic monument, related to the First Dacian War (less probably to both the first and second wars) and who associate it with the notion of revenge for the Fuscus and Sabinus disasters. If this view is right, its comparison with the Column is obviously a matter of vital necessity for solving the problems involved.

To understand when and why the Tropaeum was built at Adamklissi and was dedicated to the avenging war-god, another hypothesis should be taken into account. During the First Dacian War the standards lost by Fuscus' army (probably at Adamklissi) were recovered (Dio, LXVIII, 9, 3) and this was, for the Romans, a most suitable occasion for dedicating a trophy *Marti Ultori*. The temple of Mars Ultor in Rome had, in fact, been dedicated by Augustus to mark the recovery of Roman standards from the Parthians *(signis Parthicis receptis)*.

From the artistic point of view, one is inclined to think that the striking 'roughness' of the 'metopes' reliefs is due to the stylistic limitations of mid-imperial provincial workmanship, rather than to late-imperial decadence. But this unsophisticated style, as we shall see, may be regarded as an asset, rather than as a defect, since it preserves the spontaneity of first-hand documentation.

The scenes on the Column above the ashes of the *Optimus Princeps* in Rome, conceived by a great artist and elaborated in official symbolism, are a wonderful work that has transmitted to us the 'epos' of Trajan's glories. At Adamklissi, on the other hand, the individual panels, set up near the cenotaph of the fallen soldiers (Dessau, *ILS* 9107, see p. 50), confined by the limits of their frames and realistic in their style, make us perceive directly the human 'pathos' and cruelty experienced in the Dacian wars, here stripped of any commemorative idealization and therefore more touching. But both in Rome and at Adamklissi, the *exercitus* with Trajan at its head always represents the means and the aim of the commemorations. That is why the two monuments, equally noble in their respective forms if unequal in their styles, complement one another so well.

With the aid of the Tropaeum and of the Column, we shall now go 'on campaign' with the Roman army, trying to recognize its troops, to see its enemies face-to-face, and to observe its weapons and way of fighting. The chronological order of events, established on the Column's spirals, will help us to control the order recently attributed to the 'metopes' (Florescu), an order which must remain a matter for discussion, since none of them was preserved in its original place.

The scenes in the individual 'metopes' will be found to give hints of their places in the sequence of historical events. Representations drawn from other sources will also prove to be of help.

From the 'metopes' it is not possible to conjecture the course of the Roman advance in the Banat (as has been attempted from the Column; see Davies), namely the crossing of the Danube at Viminacium and the march of Trajan along the route towards Tibiscum. *Fig. iii*

The first seven 'metopes' contain all the cavalry engagements that appear in the series. The cavalry did actually play an important role in the initial advance, which must have been rapid if it is true that many Dacian fortresses on the above mentioned route had been evacuated (cf. Davies); but it is quite unlikely, nor is it suggested on the Column, that the cavalry thereafter left the stage. The riders represented in the 'metopes' probably belong to auxiliary *alae*; they wear the *lorica hamata* (chain-mail), unusual on Trajan's Column.

'Metope' IX could be interpreted as an *adlocutio*, while the following 'metopes', where *signiferi, bucinatores* and legionaries are seen at first drawn up in line and then in battle (as far as 'metope' XXVII), might well represent an important battle, 22 perhaps that at Tapae. The equipment of the Roman infantry is in part different from that represented on Trajan's Column: it is, in fact, closer in many respects to the equipment seen on the reliefs of the Column of Marcus Aurelius. The *lorica segmentata* is completely absent on the 'metopes', its place being taken by the *squamata* or the *hamata*; the *cingulum militiae* is also absent. The shields are oval or tile-shaped, while the helmet is of the conical, ribbed type. The above-mentioned deviations from the dress of the soldiers on Trajan's Column, have been sometimes invoked in order to challenge the Trajanic date of the 'metopes' in favour of a later one. It must be borne in mind, however, that on the Column the details of the armour are strongly stereotyped, for they were not so much intended to be wholly realistic as to carry a symbolic implication, in order to permit the correct recognition and commemoration of the different troops of Trajan's army (legionaries, *auxilia*, etc.; see below).

On the other hand, the foe is represented on the 'metopes' with a much greater wealth of detail as regards costumes,

22 'Metope' XXVII. A Roman soldier in action between two Dacian warriors (the one on the left with a cap), both of whom are armed with great scythes; at a higher level lies the corpse of a barbarian with long hair and outstretched arms, which hang down as if from a steep hill-slope (mountain fighting?).

weapons, and ethnographical features than he is on the Column; such details have been obviously well assimilated by the provincial artist. There the Dacians are often represented as stripped to the waist, or (especially the prisoners) as wearing tunics or 'shirts' of various shapes, pleated *bracae*, characteristic boots and headgear. Frequent on the 'metopes' is the hair-style with a lateral knot, which on Trajan's Column is found only in the case of one personage, a barbarian 'ambassador', at the beginning of the Second Dacian War. This *nodus*, mentioned by many ancient authors (Seneca, Tacitus, Ammianus Marcellinus, Silius Italicus) as being distinctive of some Germanic people, has been held to corroborate the thesis that we are not dealing here with Dacians and therefore not with Dacian wars, but with battles against the Bastarnae and the Roxolani ('metope' XXI). It is, however, well known that these tribes

90–1

23 'Metope' XXVIII. Badly damaged like the other metopes of Adamklissi, which are in a crude and realistic provincial style.

were in alliance with the proper Geto-Dacians in the great wars. Moreover, Florescu has demonstrated, with sound ethnographical arguments, that some elements of the attire represented on the 'metopes' have survived in Transylvanian folklore.

Taking up again the sequence of the 'metopes', we find at 'metope' XXVIII the figure of a high-ranking Roman officer on horseback running over, and thrusting his spear at, a Dacian: this may well be Trajan himself, in an attitude officially represented on the relevant coinage, but not on the Column. This 'metope' indicates the victorious conclusion either of a campaign or of the entire First Dacian War, to be followed by the opening of the Second War (Picard), since later on there is again a group of *signiferi* (XXIX), an *adlocutio* (XXXI), a *decursio* with praetorians (?) and a formation of

23

13

24 'Metope' XXXVI. Trajan and two infantrymen. Compare *31–2*

legionaries in combat. Trajan is definitely to be identified on 'metope' XXXVI wearing an elaborate moulded cuirass and a kilt with three rows of *pterygia*; he is marching into a forest, followed by two infantrymen.

A scene worth attentive consideration is also carved on 'metope' XXXIV: a Roman soldier arrives at a place where a mouldering corpse (almost a skeleton) lies; there is a typical *gladius* in the background, showing the corpse to be that of a Roman, and a Dacian archer, naked, aims his arrow at the advancing Roman from a tree. Such a scene recalls that described by Tacitus (*Ann.* I; 61, 62) when Germanicus arrived at a place strewn with the bones of Varus' legionaries, slaughtered five years before. It could represent either an ambush in the woods, or hint at the arrival of Trajan's soldiers on the field of Fuscus' disaster and at the Romans' vengeance.

25 'Metope' XLIII. A battle among wagons. A Roman soldier stands on a wagon, where a Dacian woman sits in a suppliant attitude, and thrusts his spear into the shoulder of a Dacian warrior on the ground below; in the corner lies the corpse of a slaughtered child.

This and the subsequent scenes ('metopes' XXXV–XLIII) are of particular interest, since they show features suggestive of events more explicitly represented on Trajan's Column.

The march (a ride on the Column) of Trajan at the head of light-armed troops, and the fights in a woody and hilly district, are almost identical on both monuments. In particular, on 'metopes' XL–XLIII, a battle among wagons is represented (reminiscent of the American Wild West) and it is clearly related to an analagous scene on the Column.

It should be emphasized that the battle among the wagons and the combats on the hills are represented in Rome as taking place, not during the Second, but during the First Dacian War, in connection with the diversion-campaign in Lower Moesia. On the other hand, no historical document informs us of a battle of so special a character that it merited commemoration

25

33–4

on both monuments. The wagons are four-wheeled and carry luggage, women and children, as well as Dacian warriors (on *33–4* the 'metope') and even the fluttering 'dragon' (on the Column), as though to signify that this is a tribal migration and not merely a Dacian military formation crushed by the Romans.

As regards battles in the mountains, it is well known that Dacian resistance was centered on fortified hill-tops in the south-western Transylvanian Alps. There took place the final *58–64* struggles of the first war, as represented on the Column. The fighting there was very severe, suggesting to the artist of Adamklissi the macabre scenes of corpses stretched upon a slope, or placed high up so as to almost dominate the fighters *22* ('metopes' XXXV, XXXVII).

A peculiar scene follows, that of a herd of rams fighting (XLIV). Then come the *decursio* of the victorious troops with the *vexilliferi* (probably auxiliary), the legionaries and the *auxilia* (?) already mentioned, a double scene of *adlocutio*, the prisoners and, finally 'metope' LIV showing barbarian women and children.

As to weapons and their use, the 'metopes' provide evidence *22* of the large 'battle-scythe', wielded with both hands by the Dacians and quite different in size and use from that repro- *32, 10* duced on Trajan's Column and coinage. Indeed, much later we find the same large scythe held by an auxiliary, obviously a Dacian, belonging to the guard of Marcus Aurelius, on his Column, and carved on an inscription set up by the *cohors I Aelia Dacorum* at Birdoswald in Cumberland (*RIB*, 1914). The Roman *pila*, lost on Trajan's Column, are well preserved on the 'metopes'. Moreover, the *gladius* is often used point downwards to jugulate the enemy, as also on the Column of Marcus Aurelius, a detail which Vegetius confirms. In the experience of the *exercitus* in the Dacian wars the traditional superiority of the short Roman thrusting dagger, compared with weapons used for cutting, was evidently put to a very hard test by the long and extremely violent edgeblow of the Dacian scythe.

Vegetius (I, 12) declares that the Romans, equipped with their *gladii*, get easily the better of the enemy, which faces them with long, cutting weapons. However, from the vivid pictures of Adamklissi, one obtains a completely different impression!

On the whole, the 'metopes' of the Tropaeum Traiani can be said to transmit a simple and clear message, suited to the

64

provincial public to whom it was mainly addressed, in which the superiority in war of the Roman *miles* over the barbarian warrior is stressed. Nevertheless, as on the Column, so here, a great tribute is paid to the courage and sacrifice of the Dacians.

Owing to the simplicity of its picture-language, the Tropaeum has no place for the ceremonies and more complicated fieldworks that play a major role on the Column's frieze.

To sum up, at Adamklissi the only scenes that can be connected with 'history' seem to be related, as has been already said, to the First Dacian War. This suggests the interesting possibility of changing the order of other 'metopes', moving them from the supposed Second to the First Dacian War and holding that the whole series of 'metopes' is related to the first war alone.

26 All the components of the Roman army go into action. A legionary or praetorian (lower right) with drawn dagger, covering himself with his tile-shaped shield, is backed by an auxiliary infantryman who displays the shield emblem of a unit of *civium Romanorum ingenuorum* or *singulares* (Fig. vii, no. 6); in front, another bearded auxiliary shows the shield-emblem of a gallant unit *torquata* (Fig. viii, no. 16). Two long-haired and bearded barbarian-looking *symmachiarii* are above.

CHAPTER III

THE ROMAN ARMED
FORCES IN
TRAJAN'S TIME

WHEN CONFRONTED with the military scenes which predominate on Trajan's Column, one needs some knowledge of the fundamental facts concerning the organization and general characteristics of the Roman army and navy in order to appreciate them.

I now propose to present a sketch of the Roman army and navy as they were in Trajan's epoch. This should make it possible for the amateur, no less than the student, to recognize precisely what is represented in the Column's military scenes, to pick up the clue to the meaning of single incidents or of whole episodes, to understand the renderings of details of inanimate objects, the role of participators in the actions, and the changing backgrounds. Anyone who wants to broaden his knowledge of particular aspects of the subject, more or less closely related to the Column, should consult the specialized books referred to in the text and listed in the Bibliography.

THE ROMAN IMPERIAL ARMY

Composition and strength

The Roman imperial army *(exercitus)* was subdivided into what might be described as 'field' and 'garrison' units (legions and auxiliaries), 'guards' (praetorians and *singulares*) and 'police' *(urbaniciani)*. To the great 'army of the field' some units of the 'guards' were often attached, especially when the emperor was at the theatre of war in person.

In Trajanic times this great army was composed of thirty legions, two of which were recruited by Trajan himself *(legio II Traiana Fortis* and *legio XXX Ulpia Victrix)*, of ten praetorian cohorts, of four urban cohorts, and of about 300 auxiliary units. The land forces of Rome were thus about 400,000 men strong, numbering 180,000 legionaries, 5,000 praetorians, 6,000 *urbaniciani* and over 200,000 auxiliaries. They made up by far the greatest professional army that the world had seen before the First World War.

Conditions of service

The army was of a 'professional' or 'permanent' type; the recruits *(tirones)* were enlisted (by *dilectus*) as volunteers or by press-levee (a process which was also adopted in recently conquered territories for auxiliary units), at an average age of 17–22 years. The picked recruits underwent a medical examination *(probatio)* and, if found fit for service, were incorporated for the following periods of service: for at least 25 years in the legions and in the auxiliary units; for 16–25 years in the praetorian and urban cohorts.

In the Trajanic epoch it was still necessary for those joining the legions and the praetorian and urban cohorts to possess the Roman citizenship. Recruitment for the legions was mostly from Roman citizens in the provinces, while in the praetorian and urban cohorts Italians and 'Romans' in the strict sense predominated.

Enlistment in the auxiliary units was open to the free *peregrini* of the provinces as well as to non-provincial 'barbarians', all lacking the Roman citizenship.

Soon after the famous defeat of Quinctilius Varus (AD 9), Augustus hastily put together thirty-odd auxiliary cohorts of Roman citizens *(voluntariorum civium Romanorum)* in order to compensate for the sudden loss of three whole legions in Germany.

These auxiliary units of Roman citizens remained among the ordinary auxiliaries, together with other regiments of Italians *(ingenuorum, Campanorum)*. Meanwhile, the title of *civium Romanorum* was granted to several auxiliary units as a reward for merit. All the afore-mentioned units were, however, regularly replenished with non-Roman recruits, as was the case with the auxiliaries in general.

At the beginning of their service the men took the military oath *(sacramentum)*; at its expiration *(stipendiis emeritis)* they were given an honourable discharge *(honesta missio)*, but, if unfit (owing to wounds or illness), they were liable to discharge at any moment *(missio causaria)*. For serious misconduct they could be expelled from the army *(ignominiosa missio)*. The veterans could be kept in, or recalled to *(evocati)*, service. The auxiliary soldiers, on their demobilization, received a diploma (a double bronze tablet; see p. 50) granting the Roman citizenship to themselves, to their legitimate wives and to their sons (by *conubium*). Before the expiration of the 25 years of service *(ante emerita stipendia)* such a privilege was sometimes bestowed upon individual men, as well as upon entire units, as a reward for outstanding gallantry. Similar bronze discharge-diplomas, with a different type of inscription, were given to the praetorians, but none were issued to the legionaries.

The annual pay *(stipendium)* was about 300 *denarii* for the legionaries, 1,000 for the praetorians, 500 for the *urbaniciani*, 150(?) for the auxiliary cavalrymen and 75–100 for the auxiliary infantrymen. The non-commissioned and the commissioned officers received pay that was from two to forty times higher than that of the rank and file. Sums for equipment and food were deducted from the pay. Proportional grants (in money or in land) were awarded on discharge; and special gifts *(donativa)* were also bestowed by the emperor after victories, or by will, but only to those soldiers who possessed the Roman citizenship.

In Trajan's time began the enlistment in the Roman army of irregular barbarian troops, who kept their own weapons, dress and customs. These *symmachiarii* (literally 'fighting-with') were subdivided into sections of 300 men each, under the command of a Roman *praefectus* (or *praepositus*). Under Hadrian and the Antonines such sections gained further importance and were named *numeri*. On discharge their men did not acquire, as the regular auxiliaries did, the right of becoming Roman citizens.

The administration of the very complex and far-flung Roman military forces, especially as regards the most important matters, was centralized in Rome. For instance, each one of the discharge-diplomas, distributed in thousands to auxiliary soldiers stationed on the distant frontiers of the empire, was engraved in Rome, and the exact location of the official copy of the law which authorized the grant was duly noted in the text.

Organization

As in modern armies, the units of the Roman forces were designated by numbers and by special names *(cognomina)*. The ordinal number could be common to various legions (for instance: *legio I Italica, legio I Minervia, legio I Adiutrix)* because of the splitting up of the army during the civil wars. The names, in the case of legions, may be reminders of the province in which the unit had distinguished itself, or of the emperor who founded it, or they could indicate the legion's quality *(Fortis, Fulminata, Firma,* etc.).

In the case of auxiliary units, there was, as well as the number, a *cognomen* that often indicates the ethnic origin, or more rarely the name of the Roman founder *(Petriana, Siliana,* etc.). To the number and to the first *cognomen* other titles could be added as an award of honour [*pia fidelis (p.f.)* etc.] or of further imperial favour *(Ulpia, Flavia,* etc.). Some auxiliary units bore names alluding to their decorations *(dona militaria,* see p. 79), e.g., *torquata* or *bistorquata,* or *torquata armillata.*

It has already been mentioned that the title of *civium Romanorum (c.R.)* could be granted to whole auxiliary units as a reward for special merit, if the unit itself did not belong to those already composed of Romans or Italian *ingenui.*

In the case of the auxiliary regiments there were also titles indicating specialization, e.g. *sagittariorum, funditorum, contariorum, scutata,* etc.; the numerical strength *milliaria* or *quingenaria*; and the possible presence either of a mounted squadron in an infantry regiment *(cohors equitata)* or of infantrymen in a cavalry regiment *(ala peditata).*

It is, however, necessary to recall that in Trajan's time many auxiliary units had already lost the ethnological composition indicated by their original names, since the recruiting for these named units had been extended to men from different countries. Nevertheless, in the case of the British units *(alae* and *cohortes Brittonum)* the custom of recruiting exclusively from the motherland seems to have obtained for a long time. This is also true of the specialized auxiliary troops, particularly of the archers, who generally came from the oriental provinces which produced the most skilled bowmen.

The legion

The legion, the basic and classic unit of the Roman army, was about 6,000 infantrymen strong, with a small body of 120 horsemen, who acted as signalmen and escort-corps. The legion was sub-divided into ten cohorts; and a cohort was, in turn, composed of three maniples of two centuries each. Thus, in a legion there were sixty centuries and thirty maniples. It is a matter of debate whether, in the legion of the Middle Empire, the maniple (Parker, p. 42) or the century (Passerini, 1950, pp. 550, 551) should be regarded as an administrative, rather than a properly tactical unit. The fact that each maniple had a standard of its own, while it is uncertain that the century had one, makes it more likely that the maniple, and not the century, had a position of particular importance when it came to the drawing up of the legion on the battlefield.

The centuries, about a hundred men strong, were sub-divided into squads *(contubernia)* of eight soldiers each. The *cohors* had an average strength of 600 men, but it is probable that the 1st cohort *(primus ordo)* had a higher number of soldiers than the 10th.

Each legion was an autonomous unit and, as such, comprised technicians of the engineer corps *(fabri)*, a medical corps, and personnel responsible for provisions, transport and various other services. The fighting men were always supported by an administrative organization.

The commander of the legion was a *legatus (legatus legionis)* of senatorial rank, aided by a staff of five or six military tribunes *(laticlavii, angusticlavii, semestres)* of senatorial or equestrian rank, who were at the head of the various *officia* (services) of the complex legionary unit. Besides the *legatus* there was the *praefectus castrorum*, who was in charge of the organization and administration of the legionary quarters and who served several legions when two or more shared a camp.

The command of the cohorts was entrusted to the senior centurions. It is probable that in Trajan's time the strength of the 1st cohort had already been increased to 1,000 men, under five centurions only.

The problem of rank among legionary centurions is an intriguing one (see Parker, pp. 32–5) and only an outline will be given of it here. In each cohort (of six centuries) there were, in hierarchical order, two *centuriones pilarii (pilus prior* and *pilus posterior)*, two *centuriones principes (prior* and *posterior)*, and two *centuriones hastati (prior* and *posterior)*. This order was somewhat reminiscent of the original drawing up of the republican legion into lines *(ordines)*. The highest ranking centurion was the *primipilus*, i.e. the *pilus prior* in the 1st cohort. It is uncertain, however, if the ranking of the other centurions followed the numeration of the cohorts from the 1st up to the 10th, or if the *centuriones pilarii* of every cohort ranked higher than all the *centuriones principes* and *hastati*. As *centuriones primi ordinis* the senior ones should be equated, in general, with the *pilarii* of the 1st cohort or, perhaps, with all the centurions in this cohort. In the above-mentioned reformed cohort (at any rate in the 1st), containing 1,000 men, it seems that the *primus pilus posterior* was abolished, while a second *primipilus* appeared on the legionary staff *(primus pilus bis)*. The presence of sixty centurions within a legion remained constant.

Below the rank of centurion there were junior and non-commissioned officers with the title of *principales*, divided into *beneficiarii* and *immunes* for military and 'clerical' tasks *(officia)*. This subdivision (Domaszewski) of the *principales* has been recently discussed (Dobson, p. vi); and it has been pointed out that originally the *principales* were only entrusted with tasks and did not have proper ranks, whereas from Trajan's time onwards both tasks and a rank were assigned to them. During the Late Empire the situation of the *principales* seems to be confused, since Vegetius (II, 7) states that all the legion's officers were *principales*, while in the *Digest* (L 6, 7, 6) the *principales* are reckoned among the *immunes*. At any rate, in Trajan's time the term 'rank' could be properly used of the following: *aquilifer*, who was entrusted with holding the legion's emblem and ranked just below a centurion; *optio* or understudy for the centurion, and *optio ad spem* (looking forward to *primi ordines*) in the case of the better qualified; *signifer*, who held the emblem of an individual unit (maniple or century); *tesserarius*, who gave the password; *custos armorum*, entrusted with the armoury of each century. It is doubtful whether the *imaginifer*, who held the image (of the emperor or of a unit), was considered equal in rank to the *signifer*. However, in an important inscription relevant to the Dacian wars (at Adamklissi), the *imaginiferi* are listed together with the *signiferi* and *optiones* (*ILS* 9107).

Beneficiarii and *immunes* were appointed to various tasks in the smaller units. The rank and file were named *gregales* or simply *milites*. Administrative appointments were those of *fru-*

mentarius (chief of supplies), who could also be a centurion, of *architectus* (engineer), *mensor* (surveyor), *librarius* (book-keeper), *notarius* (clerk), *medicus, veterinarius*, etc.

As regards the *medici*, denoting the whole Roman army medical corps, the rank of *principalis* was held by the better qualified *medicus ordinarius*, who could have specialized as a *clinicus, chirurgus*, or *veterinarius*; by the *capsarii*, entrusted with the first-aid kit *(capsa* means, literally, the medico-pharmaceutical *apotheke)*; and by the *optio* and *librarius valetudinarii*, the administrative officers of the military hospital. Some of the *medici* could rise to the centurionate *(iatros ekatontarkos: coh.I praetoria Lusitanorum equitata;* see Rossi, 1969), or be *immunes*; and even simple *milites* could serve as orderlies *(milites medici, discentes capsarii*, etc.).

In the administrative branch the *cornicularius* (adjutant) was a sort of petty officer. The military police was probably represented by the *statores*. There were, also, official interpreters in the legion; we know the name of the interpreter for the Dacian language in the *legio I Adiutrix* (Passerini, 1950).

In view of the importance attached to military works on the Column's reliefs, it is useful to remember that the rank of *praefectus fabrum*, the chief engineer, was a very high one, if not very well defined, and it often led to successive appointments in the fleet or in the civil service.

Very important, mainly for the transmission of orders, were wind-instruments, so often represented on the Column: the *bucina* and *cornu* (curved horns), and the *tuba* (straight trumpet) were played by the military musicians *(aeneatores)* called, according to the instruments that they played, *bucinatores, cornicines*, or *tubicines*. The band of the legion was composed of 37 *tubicines*, 35 or 36 *cornicines* and 12 *bucinatores*, distributed as follows: the first *tubicen* (with the rank of *optio*) was attached to the legionary commander, and the second to a tribune *(semestris)*; 5 *tubicines* and 5 *cornicines* were assigned to the 5 centuries of the 1st cohort, while another 30 *tubicines* and 30 *cornicines* were assigned one to each maniple; 3 *tubicines* and 3 *cornicines* belonged to the legionary cavalry. One *bucinator* was assigned to each cohort and to the legionary cavalry. All the musicians (except the above-mentioned first *tubicen*) held the rank of *immunes*. The *tuba* gave to the soldiers the signals of march, rest, beginning of the watch, etc., while the *cornu* and the *bucina* transmitted the orders to the standards and gave the most important signals on the battlefield. In the presence of the emperor, or at the execution of capital sentences pronounced by military courts, the *classicum* was played, a traditional tune of Republican ancestry.

Finally, the cavalry of the legion, a small body of 120 *equites* divided into *turmae* (of about 40 horsemen each), was led by *decuriones*. The commander of the legionary cavalry was a tribune, sometimes the *semestris*.

Praetorian and urban cohorts

The praetorian cohort of the imperial guard was 500 men strong, divided into three maniples and six centuries. Each cohort had a cavalry section of ninety *equites praetoriani* divided into three *turmae*. There were also special foot and mounted troops called *speculatores*, enrolled with the praetorian cohorts, but their number is uncertain. The general command of the praetorians was entrusted to the *praefectus praetorius* of equestrian rank, whereas the individual cohorts were led by a tribune *(tribunus cohortis)* with a staff of six military tribunes, one *laticlavius* of senatorial rank, and five of equestrian rank. Such a system of command was precisely similar to that of the legion. There were, as usual, the centurions whose *primi ordines* are mentioned without any evidence for the distinction between *pilus, hastatus* and *princeps*; the senior praetorian centurion seems to have been the *centurio trecenarius*. Below ranked the *principales*, the *optiones*, the *signiferi* (there was no *aquilifer*) and the same other junior and non-commissioned officers as in the legion. However, the praetorian soldier enjoyed a higher position than the legionary; and in the hierarchy of ranks the prestige of the praetorian one was greater than the corresponding rank in the legions.

The urban cohorts, originally intended to serve as guards in Rome *(in custodiam urbis)* and eventually also stationed at Ostia, Puteoli and Lugdunum (Lyons), were each 1,500 men strong and organized like the praetorian cohorts.

The auxilia

The auxiliary troops were subdivided into *alae* (regiments of cavalry) and *cohortes* (regiments of infantry), 500 or 1,000 men strong (*ala* and *cohors quingenaria* or *milliaria*, respectively). A very few cavalry *alae* had some foot-soldiers incorporated in them *(ala peditata)*, while numerous infantry cohorts had a mounted section *(cohors equitata)*. Cavalrymen, who had been selected from the *auxilia*, were drafted into the *alae singularium* to serve as an imperial bodyguard, whose tasks were similar to those of the praetorians.

It must, however, be pointed out that, in connection with the Trajanic army campaigning in Dacia, the term *pedites singulares (Britannici)* has been applied *(CIL* XVI, 57), unconvincingly, to irregular troops of the type of the *numeri* already mentioned.

Semi-barbarian auxiliary units of this kind were at that time called *symmachiarii*, not *singulares*; and an Asturian unit of this class is known to have fought in Dacia, under the command of a prefect (see p. 54).

The *ala quingenaria* of auxiliary cavalry was divided into sixteen *turmae*, of about thirty men each; the *ala milliaria* into twenty-four *turmae*. The commander of the *ala* had the title of prefect *(praefectus alae)*, while the *turmae* were led by *decuriones* (with *duplicarii* and *sexquiplicarii*), the senior of whom was the *decurio princeps*; below ranked, among the *principales*, the *optio* and the *vexillarius alae*, the *signifer* and *vexillarius turmae*, the *imaginifer*, the *custos armorum*, the *curator*, the *cornicularius*, etc.

The auxiliary *cohors quingenaria* was divided into six centuries, the *cohors milliaria* into ten, each of 80 to 100 men, in turn subdivided into *contubernia*, eight men strong.

The commanding officer of a *cohors quingenaria* held the title of prefect, whereas a *milliaria* was led by a tribune; this latter title was granted to the commanders of the *cohortes voluntariorum c.R., ingenuorum c.R., Italica c.R., Campestris* and, very probably, *prima Campanorum voluntaria*.

The centuries were led by centurions, the senior being the *centurio princeps* (no *primi ordines* existed); the junior ranks were those already mentioned.

The *cohors equitata quingenaria* was composed of 600 infantry (six centuries) and 120 horsemen (four *turmae*); the *milliaria* of 760 infantry (ten centuries) and 240 horsemen (eight *turmae*). These riders *(equites cohortales)* ranked below the regular cavalrymen of the *alae (equites alares)*.

In the *auxilia*, as well as in the legions, there were the trumpeters and horn-blowers *(tubicines, cornicines* and *bucinatores)*;

the medical service was entrusted to the *medici ordinarii* and to the *medici* (doctors).

In Trajan's time all the officers in the auxiliary units had still to possess the Roman citizenship. The ranks in the *auxilia* were, as has been seen, somewhat lower in prestige than the corresponding ones in the legions.

In the course of their military career the Roman officers often passed through various ranks and *officia* from the legions to the praetorian and urban cohorts, and to the auxiliaries and vice versa. Likewise the auxiliary soldiers could be transferred to a legion; the transfer of a legionary to an auxiliary unit was, however, rather rare and, perhaps, of punitive significance.

Vexillationes

Single detachments were detailed from legions, praetorian cohorts and, more rarely, from auxiliary units to be employed in operations that were sometimes far distant from their bases. The detachment was called a *vexillatio*, and it was under the command of an officer who was of higher or lower rank according to the contingent's composition. The employment of *vexillationes* alongside of entire units, which was already quite extensive in Trajanic time, was destined to increase in scale in later periods.

Camps and quarters

The individual legions were quartered in large permanent camps in the different provinces. The sites of these fortresses sometimes retain even today the name, plan and relics of the legionary quarters (Caerleon, Leon, Aosta, etc.). The permanent camp followed, more or less strictly, the standard outline of the *castrum*, which was built very precisely and rapidly by the soldiers at the halting-places, when a legion was moved or was taking part in a military campaign. Its shape was quadrangular and it was surrounded by a ditch and a mound *(vallum)*. Its four gates, one on each side, were protected by *claviculae* (curved sections of wall projecting inwards); and it had two streets, at right angles to one another *(decumanus* and *cardo)*, which began at the gates and divided the camp into four main parts, further sub-divided by criss-cross parallel minor roads. At the centre there was the large tent of the commander *(praetorium)*, near which were the tents of the tribunes *(tentoria)*, while smaller and simpler leather tents *(papiliones)* sheltered the legionaries of each *contubernium*. The standards were also sheltered in a tent adjoining the *praetorium*.

The praetorians were quartered in Rome, in the *Castra Praetoria* on the Viminal Hill. The *auxilia* were generally distributed along the empire's frontiers. Single units occupied *castella*, minor permanent camps or forts, whose plan was similar to the legionaries' *castra*. The camps occupied by cavalry units or *cohortes equitatae* showed some differences. The remains of many *castella* of these border-troops *(limitanei)* are still well preserved, as on the Hadrianic and Antonine walls in Britain. Smaller detachments of *auxilia* (or of *numeri*) garrisoned small forts and control- and signalling-towers built along the *limes* at regular intervals. The *singulares imperatoris*, like the praetorians, were quartered in Rome (*Castra Peregrinorum* on the Caelian Hill). *1–3*

The representation of permanent or temporary camps on the Column follows a semi-conventional pattern (see Richmond). Their walls appear to be built of regular, square, masonry-like blocks, but in reality they had for the most part to be constructed with uneven stones and rocks found on the spot, or with compact blocks of turf. The different tents (*praetorium,* *tentoria, papiliones*, etc.) are often shown inside the camps. *9, 16, 52* *127*

Technical works

It should be emphasized that both the preparation of defensive or offensive works (war machines, etc.) and the construction of roads, bridges, and masonry and wooden buildings, excavations, etc., more or less directly connected with the military apparatus, were in the hands of the legionaries (and praetorians) and sometimes (perhaps to a lesser degree) of the *auxilia*. All such works were under the supervision of the legionary 'military engineers' (*praefecti fabrum, architecti*, etc.).

As can be clearly seen on the Column's reliefs, technical skill in construction has a place as important as that enjoyed by destructive power in battle in the commemoration of the Roman spirit and military virtues. The ideal qualities of the *miles* were not only bravery, strength and discipline, but also intelligence, craftsmanship and ability for organization. For the attainment and perfection of these qualities there was provided a continuous and severe training with arms and tools, in manoeuvre and in construction; the word *exercitus*, which designates Roman military forces, is linked not only etymologically, but in actuality, with 'exercise'. This is perhaps the main cause of the outstanding distinction and superiority of the *exercitus Romanorum* compared with all the other 'armies' of antiquity.

Battle formations

Under the Republic the battle formation of the Roman army was based on the deployment of the legion in three lines *(ordines)*, with cavalry covering the wings *(alae)*, but it underwent many detailed changes of structure in the course of the centuries. Julius Caesar commonly used the three lines *(triplex acies)*, with four cohorts in the first line and three in the second and third lines, though on occasions he used a *duplex acies*. Detailed information about the formations of the early Empire is scanty, and in Trajan's time the rules for the employment and drawing up of the legions (and of the *cohortes praetoriae*) in battle did not always follow a tight scheme. But the concept of 'row' or *ordo* remained, being inherent in the very concept of the legion itself, which, as a great military unit, was the best fitted to engage in pitched battles of major importance by deploying its troops with precision (where possible) on an open, flat field with few natural obstacles.

Reference has been made to this concept of 'alignment' of the legion, so as to make it clear that, on Trajan's Column, the legionaries more than once appear drawn up in a row for the
61   fight, while such a formation is less frequent for *auxilia*.

Here, too, seems to lie the original reason for the adoption and development of the auxiliary troops themselves as an element in the Roman army, namely the two fundamental and insuperable defects of the legions: the rigid way in which they were drawn up, and the character of their equipment. In fact, the heavy legionary infantry was not suited to fighting on a hilly and uneven terrain; and in its early days it lacked the specialized units of archers, slingers, etc. Moreover, the decline of the legionary cavalry must also be taken into account. The result of this was that in imperial times nearly all the mounted formations belonged to the *auxilia*.

The *auxilia* do not seem ever to have been tied to fixed and rigid schemes of array, apart from those demanded by the

78

characteristics and specialities of the individual formations. Their subdivision into units of 500–1,000 men made them very easy to use either singly or *en masse*, as the need arose. The same may, perhaps, be said for the legionary or praetorian *vexillationes*, whose presence in the theatre of war became more and more important during the imperial epoch.

Last came the *symmachiarii* (and some Trajanic *pedites singulares*?), who retained customs, arms (for example, the wooden club), and battle techniques (including the war shout) that we might call 'tribal' and who often appear hurling themselves into a savage fray at the side of the *auxilia* in scenes on the Column.

One can nevertheless deduce from one scene that even these 61 barbarians must have had a definite military training: here is seen a well-formed phalanx of *auxilia* amongst whom appears a half-naked 'irregular', in an attack on a Dacian fortress.

Among the numerous tactical devices of legionaries and *auxilia* quoted by historians (e.g. Vegetius and Arrian) we need only mention, as an example, the classic *testudo*, which is represented in a scene on the Column. This is a siege formation 62 employed for approaching the enemy's wall. The soldiers are drawn up in tightly packed lines and their shields are linked like rows of overlapping roof-tiles *(imbrices)* above their heads: the shields of the soldiers in the outer rows protect the formation's flanks.

Decorations, gifts and punishments

The *dona militaria* could be sums of money which were divided, by imperial decree, in decreasing proportions among praetorians, legionaries and, sometimes, auxiliaries of the *cohortes* and *alae civium Romanorum*.

These gifts were normally received only by soldiers who were Roman citizens. Hence, Cheesman (pp. 34, 35) has stated that the auxiliaries were excluded from the *donativa*, unless they were granted (often in the meantime) the citizenship.

Military decorations for gallantry *(praemia* or *dona militiae)* awarded by the emperor were the following: *insignia triumphalia* (triumphal standards), *corona aurea* (gold crown), *hasta pura* (silver spearhead), *vexillum* (small standard), *corona civica* (laurel crown given to one who had saved the life of a Roman citizen during a battle), *corona muralis* (for assault on a wall), *corona vallaris* (for assault on a ditch or bastion), *navalis* (in a naval or amphibious action), *obsidionalis* (in a siege), *torques* (wreath or necklace), *armillae* (armlets), *phalerae* (medallions often with the imperial portrait, worn on the cuirass). The triumphal standards were reserved for the highest ranks (governors of provinces who commanded several legions). The *vexillum* was awarded to *legati* and *tribuni*, the *hasta pura* and the *corona aurea* to centurions *(primi ordines)*, the *coronae muralis*, *vallaris*, and *navalis* to the centurions; *torques*, *armillae* and *phalerae* were awarded to the lower ranks, from centurions downwards. It must be noted that the standards of the units were also decorated with *coronae*, *torques* and *armillae*; and it is important to remember that the titles of *torquata* and of *armillata* (which is rare) were given as *cognomina* to auxiliary units for outstanding conduct in battle. These were the only titles derived from *praemia militiae*. Finally, as we have seen, for acts of bravery the Roman citizenship could be given to entire units, as well as to individual auxiliaries, before their discharge from the army *(ante emerita stipendia)*.

The punishments were divided into two groups: individual punishments and punishments for a whole unit. The former were graded according to the seriousness of the crime and ranged from a flogging given by the centurion with his stick *(vitis)* to expulsion from the army *(missio ignominiosa)* and even to capital punishment, in cases of desertion or of blatant cowardice (abandonment of the standards). The classic punishment of a whole unit (for desertion or cowardice) was the *decimatio*, that is, the putting to death of one man in every ten. The men on whom the lot fell were executed by their own fellow soldiers [cf. Rossi, 1967 (a)]. It seems that entire legions could be disbanded with the *missio ignominiosa*, that is, without *praemia emeritorum*. This could have been the case with the *legio XXI Rapax*, which disappears from history at the time of the Dacian wars (Parker, p. 114).

Military standards

31 The Roman military standards have a particular importance in that they represent not only the physical and psychological emblem of the unit and of its components, but also a basic method of transmitting orders visually to the troops. It has already been noted that sound signals were transmitted both to

individual soldiers (by the *tuba*) and to standard-bearers (by the horn and *bucina*). The standard-bearers, in turn, probably translated the sounds into the movements appropriate to the various types of manoeuvre. This method must have proved very valuable amid the uproar and confusion of the battle. From the psychological point of view, special honours and worship were given to the standards. The abandonment of standards by the soldiers, and the loss of them, especially the loss of the legionary eagle, were considered highly dishonourable and were severely punished (see above).

The standards are of three main types:

Aquila: this is the exclusive emblem of the legion. It is a golden 43, 31 eagle, with spread wings, placed at the top of a pole (bare or adorned like the *signa*) and generally perched upon a low base or on a thunderbolt (with double twisted spindle).

Signa: these are variously composed, but all derive from the 31 notion of a stake carrying different superimposed elements – round *paterae* placed vertically; *coronae* (and *torques*) placed either horizontally or vertically; lunar crescents; *imagines* (divine or imperial) set at the centre of a *phalera* or of a vertical wreath; transverse bars, plain or decorated; rectangular plates. These elements, or some of them, are variously disposed along the upper half of the stem. The lower half carries a curved projection designed to facilitate the hand-grasp and to act as a support. Since the standards were also fixed into the ground, their bottom end is pointed and carries a protrusion to prevent the pole from sinking too deeply into the earth.

At the top the *signa* bear the unit's emblem. In Trajan's time two types are to be observed: an open hand (with closed fingers), and a *corona* (or *torques*) (with a spearhead and/or a small shield). The question as to which emblems belonged to which units is still debated, and this problem will be discussed further when the Column's standards are examined. These emblems have been thought (Durry, p. 203) to be all manipular, the century and/or the cohort not having emblems of their own (under the Middle Empire). This does not seem probable, since it is hard to believe that the Romans would have attributed an identical meaning to different symbols that are often antithetical in official representations (flanking the legionary eagle on coin reverses).

81

While the *manus* clearly recalls the *manipulus*, the crown and the spearhead at the apex could have been the emblem of the cohort. For instance, on the tombstone of a standard-bearer of an auxiliary cohort *(V Asturum)* in the Bonn Museum the wreath and the spearhead are very clearly represented. The standards of the auxiliary cavalry seem to be a little different, inasmuch as they show an unadorned pole topped by a *torques* (?) encircling a spearhead or an *imago (ala Afrorum, ala Petriana)*.

Vexilla: these are square flags (of cloth) hanging from a crossbar at the top of a stake which is either bare or adorned like that of the *signa*. *Vexilla* are generally believed to be peculiar to cavalry units, but there is no doubt that they were among the standards of the cohorts of auxiliary infantry and perhaps of legionary centuries also (Vegetius). An instance of this is the *vexillarius* of the *cohors Gaetulorum* (in the Museum of Cimiez). On the other hand, we have seen that even the cavalry had *signa* of its own.

27–9 Left, the typical Roman sword (*gladius*) as represented on the Column, and below, two actual blades found at Vindonissa. Centre, a short dagger (*pugio*) and two large spearheads, together with two long 'irons' with smaller spearheads, belonging to the classic Roman javelins (*pila*).

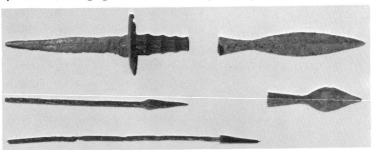

30 A Roman helmet (*galea*) of hemispherical shape.

The *vexillum* is, moreover, the typical emblem of detachments, whether praetorian or legionary or auxiliary. It is therefore not surprising to see a *vexillum* fluttering from a *signum*.

Some minor emblems were used by the legionary and auxiliary troops of the Trajanic epoch. They chiefly consist of the *imagines* of emperors or divinities, or of the animal-protector of the unit, and were carried by the *imaginifer*.

Armour, arms, and equipment

The defensive armour of the Trajanic legionary (and of the praetorian) consisted of: (1) A cuirass *(lorica)* with metal 31 bands *(segmentata)* or scales *(squamata)* applied to a leather corslet, so as to protect the thorax. (2) A metal helmet *(galea)* 30 hemispherical in shape with a reinforcement at front and back and sometimes with crossed ribs, at the top of which there was a ring (or hollow) by which a plumed crest was fixed (on parade);

the cheeks were protected by cheek pieces *(paragnathides)* hanging down at the helmet's sides. (3) A short 'kilt' of leather or cloth, sometimes strengthened by vertical metallic strips *(pterygia)* in one or two rows (according to the wearer's rank) to protect the abdomen. (4) A rectangular convex shield *(scutum)*, tile-shaped, of wood and leather, with metal reinforcements and ornaments and with various emblems and decorations on its outer face; the shield was usually carried on the left arm.

The equipment was sometimes completed by close fitting knee-breeches *(bracae)*, by military sandals (the famous *caligae*) for the soldiers, and by ankle-boots *(calcei)* for the officers. A belt with various ornaments and a large, elaborate buckle was another special mark of the Roman soldier *(cingulum militiae)*; it served as a sword-belt and was sometimes replaced by a shoulder-belt strap *(balteus)*. It is important to remember that centurions had, as a mark of their rank, a rod of command, the *vitis*.

The offensive light arms consisted of: (1) A short, pointed sword, about two feet long, with a large blade and both edges sharpened *(gladius)*, which was employed especially as a thrusting weapon and was derived from the Iberian dagger. The *gladius* had a grooved handle (to give a good grip), surmounted by a spherical or quadrangular pommel; its sheath is often finely engraved, with a metal reinforcement at bottom and top. The *gladius* was carried on the right side, hanging from the *cingulum* or *balteus*. (2) A large sharp-bladed dagger *(pugio)* with a leather sheath, which was carried on the left side, hanging from the *cingulum*. (3) A *pilum*, a javelin with a wooden shaft, within which a long point of supple iron was placed: this caused the *pilum* to bend so that it could not be extracted once it penetrated the enemy's shield or body, and if by chance the *pilum* missed its target and fell on the ground, it buckled up and was unusable by the enemy. Every legionary had two *pila* in his equipment.

The chief heavy arm of the units – one being provided for each century – was the *ballista*, a species of large crossbow, with a string held taut by two separate arms, each twisting a powerful torsion-spring placed at the sides of the latter. These springs, made with several layers of sinew cord, were wound and stretched up within two lateral drums of a composite framework (for details see Marsden). The whole engine was mounted on a tripod or carried in a special cart *(carroballista)*, supplied with a small case for ammunition and drawn by mules. The *ballistae* used by Trajan's army (Marsden, p. 43, 189) were able to throw a sturdy bolt (Baatz) for a distance of about 500 yards with remarkable accuracy and power of penetration: they were manoeuvred by a *contubernium* (squad). Big machines of this type *(onagri)*, which threw large blocks of stone or leaden balls, were built for sieges. There were, moreover, complicated siege towers mounted on wheels, and battering-rams to demolish walls: these were real masterpieces of military engineering, both in design and skill of construction. Their manipulators formed the legionary 'engineer corps'. 36

The legionary and praetorian cavalrymen probably had a lighter cuirass and helmet, a round *(parma)* or oval shield and, instead of the *pilum*, a simple javelin or the *hasta* (lance) or, sometimes, the *contus* (a heavy lance). The cavalrymen did not have stirrups or saddle. The horse had a simple saddle-cloth, reins, a bit, and more or less elaborate harness.

The auxiliary infantry generally had lighter armour. The cuirass was of chain-mail *(lorica hamata)* or was replaced by the simple leather corslet. The helmet was either of the legionary type, or conical with six to eight ribs for strengthening (the type worn by oriental archers). Sometimes a conical or shaped hat took the place of a helmet, or nothing was worn on the head. The shield, too, was light and oval. The *gladius* was generally carried, but was often replaced by a longer sword of Celtic type *(spatha)* or some special weapon (for example, a wooden club). 26

Troops with special weapons were the archers, with double-bent bows (παλίντονον τόξον) on the oriental model; the slingers; and the *scutati*, with larger tile-shaped shields. 20, 61, 100, 111 58, 109

The heavy auxiliary cavalryman was equipped with a leather corslet, a *lorica squamata* or *hamata*, an oval shield, a helmet, a *hasta* or *contus* (*contus Sarmaticus*, a heavy lance). It is interesting to note that on Trajan's Column the cavalry is generally represented without the *lorica*, while on the Adam-klissi 'metopes' cavalrymen always wear armour. The question has been discussed (Eadie) as to whether it was in Trajan's time that Rome first employed the real 'armoured cavalry' (after a Sarmato-Scythian and Parthian pattern), which was to make its official appearance in the Roman army later, under Hadrian and the Antonines *(alae cataphractatae)*.

31 A Roman legion on the march. Roman legionaries are crossing the Danube on a
bridge of boats (see also 6); they are clad in a cuirass of metal plates (*lorica segmentata*)
and carrying a quadrangular, tile-shaped shield, which is the countersign for every
legionary or praetorian on the Column; they also have a Roman sword (*gladius*) on
the belt and a helmet hanging from the right shoulder. The kit, with its various items
(pots, packs, tools, etc.), is displayed on a stake (perhaps for an inspection) borne on

e left shoulder. The emblems on the shields (laurel-crowns, see *Fig. vi*; M, N) may dicate that this is the Trajanic *legio XXX Ulpia Victrix*. The column of soldiers is eceded by the commanding officer (*legatus legionis*) wearing moulded cuirass and uble kilt, and by the standards, the flag and the legionary *aquila*, carried by the *niferi* wearing the bearskin head-dress. On the extreme right some praetorian andards are visible.

The light-armed cavalrymen, for instance, the Mauretanian cavalrymen under Lusius Quietus (which we see later on the Column), had neither helmet nor cuirass and carried a small round buckler *(caetra)* and short javelins; their horses' bridles were single.

The uniform of the auxiliaries is completed by a cloak *(sagum)* and scarf *(focale)*, garments also worn by legionaries and praetorians. Among the *auxilia* one can see various fashions of native dress and coiffure, e.g., the long fluttering tunics and the conical caps of the troops of Asiatic origin, and the simple *bracae* (short pants) of the *symmachiarii*, which left the waist bare, the short *chlamydes* and the curled hair of the Mauretanian riders.

The slingers did not have a shield or sword or body-armour, but wore a very ample tunic. On the Column's reliefs one may observe, moreover, a group of auxiliaries with a bearskin hood like that of the *signiferi* and the musicians, and another group fighting without helmets.

In fact, *signiferi, imaginiferi* and *aeneatores (tubicines, bucinatores* and *cornicines)* did not wear a helmet, but a special head-dress of bearskin (lion for the praetorian *signiferi*), the skull of the beast (without his jaw) being used as a hood, while the furry skin fell onto the shoulders and down the back and was fastened at the neck by tying the forelegs together. Further, they lacked the segmented cuirass, and wore instead a coat of chain-mail (see the Tropaeum of Adamklissi), or a leather or cloth corslet; their shields were round in shape and probably small *(parmae)*.

For resting- or marching-uniform, legionaries, praetorians and auxiliaries wore a short tunic, either sleeveless or leaving one shoulder bare, and sometimes a short cloak or cape *(paenula)*.

The kit of the Roman soldier included various tools (saw, leather strips, scythe, chain, basket and a type of pick-axe called *dolabra*), containers (dish and pot), a stock of supplies (wheat rations), a water-bottle (containing the *posca*, that is sour wine or water and vinegar), as well as clothes and, perhaps, a leather sheet for his tent. This luggage was certainly heavy to carry (Josephus; III, 5, 5).

The troops were, however, accompanied by pack-animals (mules and oxen) and by two-wheeled carts used to carry bulky

31
104

69, 76

31

items, heavy weapons and supplies *(impedimenta)*. On the Column one can see some of these carts loaded with casks and various pieces of luggage, well packed and tied up.

THE IMPERIAL NAVY

Strength and Organization

The Roman naval forces, for both sea and river service, were subdivided in Trajan's time into *classes*, each commanded by a *praefectus classis* of equestrian rank. The warships had quite large sails and oars and were classified according to the number of banks of oars or of rowers, from six *(hexeres* or admiral's ship) to three *(trieres)*. Their prows displayed a beak-like projection *(rostrum)*, surmounted by a prolongation *(proembolium)* carved with a symbol or animal and flanked by two eyes or other representations, together with the ship's name. Astern were the two parallel rudders and the aft ornament, near to which the standards and the lantern were fixed. Under the Middle *71* Empire warships were usually called *liburnae*, the name given to the lighter and swifter ships which were more and more widely employed in the navy. It should be noted that on Trajan's Column the ships with two banks of oars, which are frequently represented, are likely to be *liburnae* (Starr, p. 54). Warships were certainly accompanied by sea- and river-cargo boats and barges.

The fleets were called after their chief bases. In the Mediterranean the main naval bases were Misenum and Ravenna, and the most important fleets were the *classis Misenensis* and *classis Ravennas*, besides the fleets named *Alexandrina, Syriaca*, etc.

The provincial fleets were used partly on the sea and partly on rivers and bore the names of *classis Britannica, Germanica, Pannonica, Moesica*, etc. To the names of the individual fleets were added the usual honorific and commemorative *cognomina* *(Augusta, Flavia, praetoria, pia fidelis)*. The ships took the names of rivers *(Rhenus, Danuvius, Padus)*, of gods *(Minerva, Mercurius)*, of virtues *(Concordia, Pax)*, or of famous Greek naval battles *(Salamina)*. Hospital-ships seem to have had such suitable names as *Aesculapius* (see Rossi, 1969).

89

To every fleet were assigned, in positions of high authority, *praefecti fabrum, architecti,* and *fabri navales* (or *classici*), who were the 'naval engineers' for the design and construction, not only of ships, but also of such related works as harbours, wharfs and bridges. This is evident when one studies Trajan's Column.

It is doubtful whether the navies were subdivided into separate flotillas or naval squadrons (Starr) under the command of *navarchi,* while it is almost certain that individual units were commanded by *trierarchi.* These ranks in the navy corresponded, approximately, to the *centuriones primorum ordinum* and to the ordinary centurions of land troops respectively. The crew of every battleship corresponded to a century and was staffed by *principales, beneficiarii,* and *immunes,* as in the infantry centuries. Hence we find, in the service of a *centuria classica,* the *signifer* (who bore the *signum* of the ship or of the fleet), the *optio,* the *tesserarius,* the *armorum custos,* the *librarius,* the *secutor,* etc., as well as the *medicus* (mainly *duplicarius*), the *fabri,* and the *aeneatores (bucinatores, cornicines).* The members of the crew assigned to strictly nautical tasks, the 'real' sailors, were: the *gubernator* (helmsman), who handled the double oar-helm astern and was aided by the *proreta* who, at the bow, kept him informed of the course and of possible obstacles; the *pausarius,* who gave the rhythm to the rowers and to the *proreus* who controlled them; the *velarii,* who handled the sails.

Sailors and soldiers of the imperial fleets *(classiarii)* were enrolled voluntarily and, like the *auxilia,* were mostly free *peregrini,* often coming from the coastal provinces and lacking Roman citizenship. But officers had to be Roman citizens.

The term of service was twenty-six years. The salary was about 100 *denarii* a year (for the privates). On ordinary discharge *(honesta missio)* or on discharge for illness *(missio causaria)* the sailors received the diploma, with the guarantee of Roman citizenship and of the right of *conubium,* as the *auxilia* did.

There are many examples of single *classiarii* or bodies of them being transferred to the land army, and even of the formation of legions *(I and II Adiutrix)* by the enrolment of sailors. This occasioned (under Vespasian) judicial disputes with regard to the status of the legionaries themselves at the completion of their service. We also hear of auxiliary *alae* and *cohortes classicae.*

Finally, it should be stated that the Roman fleets not only fought in their natural element, but were also employed in amphibious operations, either by transporting contingents of the *exercitus* or by the direct participation of their own centuries and, in particular, of their technicians in the army's activities.

Armour, arms, and equipment

The armour and arms of the members of the *centuriae classicae* were probably similar to those of the legionaries. As we shall see, the Column shows some soldiers in legionary armour who must be regarded as *classiarii*. The naval uniform of the sailors seems to have been a short blouse, wide and sleeveless, which sometimes leaves one shoulder bare.

Tools were an important part of the equipment of the *classiarii*. When rendered in art these emphasize the sailors' special role as 'carpenter engineers', skilled in carrying out any construction on water and particularly in making wooden structures.

In naval construction, the 'axe masters' are known to have been an elite. It would seem, therefore, that even in the land armies the most technically difficult carpentry was entrusted to the *fabri navales*, masters in the use of the axe, working under the direction of their *praefecti*, either alone or alongside the legionary *fabri*. The Column gives evidence of this.

81–2, 88, 131

CHAPTER IV

THE ARMY AND NAVY IN TRAJAN'S DACIAN WARS

Composition of the exercitus

The historical sources give us very inadequate information about the composition of Trajan's army campaigning in Dacia. On the other hand, there is a certain amount of archaeological and epigraphical material that enables us to trace, if seldom with certainty and often only by conjecture, the units which took part in the Dacian wars.

This material ranges, as usual, from commemorative and/or funerary monuments and inscriptions of legionaries and auxiliaries to simple tiles and stones with the units' names; in the case of the *auxilia* the military diplomas are of enormous help. These diplomas also supply lists of the units stationed in the neighbourhood of Dacia or in Dacia itself during or round about the period of the wars (see pp. 50–55). From this evidence it is possible to deduce which of these units were probably employed, wholly or in part, in at least one of the Dacian campaigns. The indications are that, of the neighbouring provinces liable to furnish troops for the actual theatre of war, Pannonia and Moesia (Superior and Inferior) were the chief. One would have thought, however, that the regiments stationed in Dalmatia and Thracia would have been in a better position to supply fighting units, since these, not being frontier provinces, were less exposed to external menace and therefore less in need of an army to protect them. We also find units that seem to have earned specific *cognomina* (Ulpia, Traiana) and the Roman citizenship during the actual period of the Dacian wars.

By making use of all the above factors we may attempt to compile a list of the Roman units which form the great army represented on Trajan's Column, and to record, moreover, the names of a few of their staff officers. A list of this kind can also be used for drawing comparisons and making distinctions when symbols have to be interpreted. It is also important to bear in mind that single detachments *(vexillationes)*, particularly of legionary and praetorian units, but never the entire units themselves, could have been summoned to the theatre of war.

List of the Units

LEGIONS

I Italica (tribunes: Tiberius Cl. Vitalis, Nummius Verus)
I Minervia (legate: Aelius Hadrianus in the second war)
I Adiutrix
IV Flavia Firma (*primipilus* and *praefectus castrorum*: C. Caesius Silvester in the second war)
V Macedonica (legates: L. Minicius Natalis in the first war; L. Caelius Murena in the second war; centurion: Valerius Proclus)
VII Claudia Pia Fidelis (centurion: Acanius Statura; *praefectus fabrum*: Aemilius Paternus)
XI Claudia Pia Fidelis (its employment is considered probable)
XII Fulminata (*primipilus*: Q. Raecius in the first war. Partial employment of *vexillationes*)
XIII Gemina (its employment is very probable in the second war; (tribune: C. Caelius Martialis)
XV Apollinaris (its name was inscribed in Trajan's Forum)
XX Valeria Victrix (its name was inscribed in Trajan's Forum, but its employment was partial – *vexillationes*)
XXI Rapax (its employment is to be considered probable, as is the hypothesis that the entire unit was disbanded by *missio ignominiosa* for its bad behaviour during the Dacian wars)
XXX Ulpia (formed by Trajan, was granted the title of *Victrix* in the Dacian wars; centurion: C. Silvester in the first war)

PRAETORIAN COHORTS
Under the command of Claudius Livianus, praetorian prefect, these were employed in conspicuous, but unknown numbers; the participation of the 9th cohort alone is certain.

93

Cavalry
Ala I Asturum (prefect:
  P. Prifernius Paetus)
Ala I Augusta Ituraeorum
Ala I Bosporenorum
Ala I civium Romanorum
Ala I Claudia nova
*Ala I Flavia Augusta
  Britannica milliaria c.R.*
Ala Frontoniana
Ala Gallorum Flaviana
*Ala I Hispanorum et
  Arvacorum*
Ala I milliaria
Ala I Pannoniorum
*Ala II Pannoniorum
  veterana*
Ala I praetoria singularium
*Ala Siliana c.R. torquata
  armillata*
*Ala Ulpia contariorum
  milliaria c.R.*
*Ala I Vespasiana
  Dardanorum* (prefect:
  P. Baesius Betunianus)

Infantry
Cohors I Alpinorum equitata
Cohors II Alpinorum
Cohors III Alpinorum
Cohors I Antiochensium
  (prefect: M. Calpurnius
  Sabinus)
Cohors I Arvacorum
*Cohors I Batavorum
  milliaria p.f.*
*Cohors II Batavorum
  milliaria*
Cohors I Flavia Bessorum
Cohors I Bracaraugustanorum

Cohors I Breucorum c.R.
*Cohors I Britannica milliaria
  c.R.*
*Cohors I Brittonum milliaria
  p.f. Ulpia torquata c.R.*
*Cohors II Brittonum
  milliaria equitata*
*Cohors II Brittonum
  milliaria c.R. p.f.
  (Flavia ?)*
*Cohors II Nervia Pacensis
  milliaria Brittonum*
Cohors III Brittonum
*Cohors III campestris c.R.
  (ingenuorum)*
Cohors II Chalcidenorum
Cohors I Cilicum
*Cohors I Cisipadensium
  (ingenuorum)*
*Cohors I Cretum
  sagittariorum*
Cohors IV Cypria c.R.
*Cohors III Dalmatarum
  milliaria equitata c.R.*
*Cohors II Gallorum
  Macedonica equitata*
*Cohors II Gallorum
  Pannonica*
Cohors III Gallorum
Cohors V Gallorum
Cohors VII Gallorum
*Cohors I Flavia
  Commagenorum*
*Cohors II Flavia
  Commagenorum
  sagittariorum*
*Cohors I Flavia Ulpia
  Hispanorum c.R.
  milliaria equitata*
*Cohors I Hemesenorum
  sagittariorum c.R.*

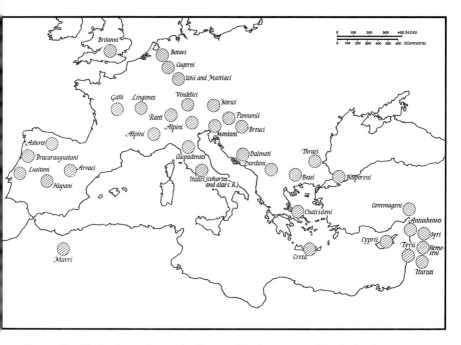

Fig. v Auxiliaries from all over the Roman Empire employed in the Dacian wars. The circles on the map indicate the places of origin and racial derivation of the auxiliary units which were summoned to the Dacian war-theatre and took part in one or both of the Trajanic campaigns.

Cohors I Hispanorum
  veterana equitata p.f.
Cohors II Hispanorum
  milliaria
Cohors II Hispanorum
  scutata Cyrenaica
  equitata
Cohors V Hispanorum
Cohors I Ituraeorum
Cohors I Augusta
  Ituraeorum
Cohors I Augusta
  Ituraeorum sagittaria
Cohors I Lepidiana c.R.

Cohors I Lingonum
Cohors I Lusitanorum
  Cyrenaica
Cohors VI Lusitanorum p.f.
Cohors II Mattiacorum
Cohors I montanorum c.R.
Cohors I Noricorum
Cohors I Pannoniorum
  veterana p.f.
Cohors IV Raetorum
Cohors VII Raetorum
Cohors I sagittariorum
  milliaria
Cohors I Sugambrorum veterana

95

Cohors I Thracum c.R.
Cohors I Thracum Syriaca
Cohors VI Thracum
Cohors I Tyriorum
Cohors I Ubiorum
Cohors I Ulpia Pannoniorum
    milliara equitata c.R.

Cohors I Ulpia Traiana
    Cugernorum c.R.
    (second war)
Cohors I Vindelicorum
    milliaria c.R.
Cohors VIII voluntariorum
    civium Romanorum

The presence of a *cohors funditorum* (slingers) is very probable.

Symmachiarii

Only the participation of one unit of *symmachiarii (Asturum)* is certain (prefect: C. Sulpicius Ursulus). Very probable is the presence of German units *(Aestii)*, as represented on the Column. Disputable is the actual participation of the *pedites singulares Britannici*. The presence of *vexillationes* of Syrian and Mauretanian light cavalry is known, the latter under the command of Lusius Quietus.

24
54-5

Staff

The high-ranking officers who are represented on the Column could be, perhaps, Licinius Sura, Q. Sosius Senecio and Aelius Hadrianus, *comites* (military advisers) of Trajan in the First Dacian War; Hadrian becomes commander of *legio I Minervia* during the second war. Claudius Livianus, the praetorian prefect, is also generally recognized.

Composition of the fleet

The Column emphasizes the prime importance of the role of the ships from the Danubian squadrons in the preparation and development of the Dacian campaigns. On the other hand, no surviving written document deals with the subject. The Column also depicts the journeys of Trajan by sea aboard ships from the Adriatic (Ravenna) fleet.

The river operations are of two main types: transport of supplies, and transport of troops (infantry and cavalry) and prisoners.

4, 5, 28-9
25

In such operations barges and cargo-boats played their part alongside the bireme and trireme warships *(liburnae)*, which were very similar to those employed at sea. These ships belonged, no doubt, to the *classis Flavia Pannonica*, based at Taurunum near Singidunum (Belgrade), and to the *classis Flavia Moesiaca*, based at Noviodunum near the mouth of the Danube.

It is likely that the non-navigable stretch of the Danube, at the Orsova Iron Gates, separated the spheres of the two squadrons. Along the upper course of the river the *classis Pannonica* received supplies from the great bases of Carnuntum and Aquincum and those sent by the main tributaries of the Danube, the Dravus (Drava) and Savus (Sava). The *classis Moesiaca* collected material and troops coming from the Black Sea or along the river Margus (Morava). The transport to, and landing in, enemy territory of men and supplies by the fleet, together with its co-operation in the construction and maintenance of bridges of boats, pontoons, and ferries, were processes that had features analogous to modern 'amphibious' operations, which demand great skill and courage.

The *coronae navales*, which were the decorations awarded for merit in operations of these types, are often seen adorning the standards of Trajan's troops on the Column and on coin-reverses (see Rossi, 1965). The emperor himself, standing at the side of the ship's pilot or on the pier nearby, directs and supervises the naval operations, thus stressing still further their *71, 30* importance.

CHAPTER V

THE REPRESENTATION OF THE ROMAN ARMY ON THE COLUMN

Introduction

It is beyond doubt that in Trajan's Column we possess an extremely rich source of information on military matters of the Middle Empire. All the same there is still a lively debate as to the exact interpretation of the reliefs, a debate which embraces the significance both of the marble scroll as a whole and of its individual scenes.

On the one hand, it has long been stated that the Column 'relates' the chronicle of the Dacian campaign (for which the literary evidence is almost completely lost), its events being ordered and presented in the documentary form of a 'triumphal cartoon'; on the other hand, recently support has been won for the theory that the monument was intended to 'emphasize' the Trajanic epic by means of a series of selected scenes specifically chosen to form a synthesis of the imperial virtues *(Virtus Augusti)* (Picard, p. 389).

These two views of the relief are, however, only opposed when carried to extremes and hence to improbable conclusions. They can be complementary to one another when seen in the light of a genuine 'Roman' concept, instead of being coloured by a modern outlook on imperial commemorative art. It is this concept which explains the use both of realistic representation and of allegorical abstraction to express a combination of 'seen' images and 'suggested' ideas; and only this can restore to the monument its original evocative power.

When embarking on the study of the reliefs from the historical standpoint, one should bear in mind [Rossi, 1966 (b)] that both the Column in Rome and the cenotaph (with the adjacent trophy) at Tropaeum Traiani must be viewed in the perspective of a great celebration of the army, with which the emperor identified himself [cf. the Younger Pliny's *Panegyric on Trajan*, 19, 3: 'sic imperatorem commilitonemque miscueras' (you combined the roles of general and comrade-in-arms)]: he dedicated the monument 'to the memory of the bravest of men who died for the republic' (see p. 50) after serving with discipline and loyalty on the Dacian expedition. On the Column, therefore, the protagonists are the soldiers, whose *res gestae* raised the *optimus princeps* to the height of apotheosis *(quantae altitudinis)* (see p. 49), displayed from the base to the top in a spiral of glory.

The theme of the spiral reliefs is centred upon the actors rather than upon the drama, with that attention to iconography and its symbolic significance which is peculiar to Roman commemorative pictures, wherein everything has its own reason, order and meaning. This principle is clearly demonstrated by the almost excessive richness and exactitude of scenes showing field engineering and military works as contrasted with the scenes of actual fighting – a contrast which raises the question of whether one is to see in the Column a concrete war documentary or, as Picard (p. 401) does, an abstract sublimation of *ponos* into *Virtus Augusti*.

This is, however, in the author's opinion, the typical Roman way of celebrating the *exercitus* in its manifold technical achievements, which were cultivated and valued as much as, or even more than, gallantry in battle. This concept of the army's activities was guaranteed by the word of the *imperator*, as stated in Hadrian's speech to the African army at Lambaesis (*ILS* 2487).

One should think of Trajan's *exercitus* as marching all round the Column's spiral band in a triumphal parade *(decursio)*, which idealizes and commemorates the Dacian wars, while showing to the onlooker a series of incidents that redound in the most effective military way to the glory of the single units, of their infantry and cavalry, and of their leader. All this is done by avoiding the lengthy narration of single episodes, and by bestowing on simple and familiar scenes the maximum of expressiveness in the minimum of space. This is well known to be the method followed in the commemorative reverse-types of the Roman coinage.

Conventional representations

It has been stressed above that the reliefs of the Column follow the conventions that are peculiar to commemorative imperial scenes in general. These conventions have been touched upon already (see p. 38). As far as the military motifs are concerned they include the rendering, in order to be concise, of one soldier, or of one standard, to symbolize an entire unit; and the same principle applies to representations of ships, buildings, camps and the like.

Turning to the more precise convention adopted in order to indicate, clearly and consistently, the main components of the Roman troops, we may note the following four 'clichés', based on dress and armament: legionaries and praetorians, auxiliaries, *symmachiarii, classiarii.*

Peculiar differences in costume and arms lead, also, to further differentiation within each of the above mentioned groups, particularly among the auxiliaries.

More complicated and uncertain, as well as more interesting, is the problem of recognizing individual units through the study of the military emblems which are represented by the standards and by the ornamental designs or badges rendered on the shields. It is important to bear in mind, in this connection, that official lists of the shield-badges, standards and colours of the Roman army were regularly issued by the imperial authority and known to the public, to judge by the *Notitia Dignitatum*, the only official list surviving (from the Late Empire).

LEGIONARIES AND PRAETORIANS

These soldiers are clearly and consistently identifiable by their 26, 31 arms and equipment. They are all clad in a metal cuirass, the *lorica segmentata* (consisting of breast- and back-plates with hoops round body and arms), and have the rectangular tile-shaped shield *(scutum)*; the belt or *cingulum militiae* is not always present. The dagger is the typical *gladius* and the helmet *(galea)* is rounded, with plates in front and behind. *Gladius* and helmet are not exclusive to legionaries and praetorians. The helmet is usually without a crest, which is worn only in some scenes of *adlocutio* (by praetorians and officers). There is a general lack of spears and lances *(pila, hastae,* etc.), which would have been applied in metal to the reliefs and are now totally lost. The soldiers are wearing a simple kilt; that of the officers and of the emperor has two superimposed rows of vertical bands *(pterygia)*. Underneath, some wear close-fitting trousers (to mid-leg); others have bare legs. All have the typical military sandals *(caligae)*. But the officers of the staff (and the emperor) have close-fitting boots *(calcei)* and a moulded cuirass; sometimes a short cloak *(sagum)* is draped over the cuirass.

The dress and arms of legionaries and praetorians are represented in a very realistic way, but the stereotyped *lorica segmentata* and, perhaps, tile-shaped shield have an evident conventional value, for the sake of exact identification. The actual 26 equipment of Trajanic legionaries and praetorians would hardly have been so absolutely 'uniform'; and it very probably comprised 'scale' and 'mail' cuirasses *(lorica squamata* and *hamata)* and large oval shields such as are represented on the 'metopes' of Adamklissi's Tropaeum, which depict the same 22, 24 soldiers in the same wars and whose date has now been quite firmly settled as Trajanic.

In a few scenes the soldiers are shown in a light camp-dress, without cuirass and arms, but wearing a sleeveless, short, and ample tunic. On the march, legionaries and praetorians carry 69 their helmets hanging from the right shoulder. While fording a 31 river the shield is held with both hands over the head as a tray 22–3 upon which cuirass and arms have been placed. The legionary kit is, in one scene, represented as suspended on a stake (a tent pole) borne on the left shoulder.

While intent on field-works, legionaries and praetorians do not have a helmet and shield, but they always wear the cuirass. Their shields are lined up nearby, resting against the spears which are planted in the earth and which have helmets suspended on top of them. It is very unlikely that the heavy and 15 cumbersome cuirass would have been so constantly worn by soldiers engaged in technical activities, but such a representation proves the overall conventional meaning of the 'cliché'. The concept had to be clearly conveyed that the legionaries and praetorians were the most renowned for their technical ability and achievements in the imperial army, with its heterogeneous forces and varied activities. The same applies to the manipulation of *ballistae* and *carroballistae*, which is entrusted only to the *contubernia* of legionaries or praetorians. Moreover, 36, 57–8 all the *ballistae* represented in the reliefs belong to a single, brand-new model, the metal-framed, dart-throwing 'Heron's *cheiroballistra*' (see Marsden, Fig. 8 and pp. 189, 190), which was presumably put into service in the army at the time of the Dacian wars. Such an exclusive representation seems to imply, again, a symbolic purpose: to give particular emphasis and credit to the technical improvements in armament which were introduced by Trajan himself. In reality, other types of *ballistae* (see p. 84) were employed at this time in the artillery of the Roman army.

AUXILIA

The main distinction between auxiliaries on the one hand, and legionaries and praetorians on the other, lies in the former's lack of the *lorica segmentata* and of the rectangular shield. For the *lorica* various kinds of armour and clothing are substituted, and
26 the shield is oval and lighter than the *scutum*. The only exceptions are a couple of auxiliary troopers with a rectangular
33 'legionary' shield, probably belonging to a *cohors scutata* (the
28 2nd *Hispanorum*?) and, perhaps, to a cohort *singularium*.

Among the auxiliaries, the ethnic and specialized traits are obviously underlined and clearly recognizable.

The archers from different countries have peculiar costumes
55, 61, 111 of at least three distinct varieties: firstly, archers with conical helmet (with or without ribs), long scale cuirass and cloak or
100 vest; secondly, archers with conical cap, without cuirass and
20 with long (double) vest; thirdly, archers equipped like the auxiliary infantrymen in general. One may suggest (see below) that the *sagittarii* of the first two varieties, dressed in a clearly oriental fashion, belonged to the following cohorts: *I Hemesenorum sagittariorum c.R., Augusta Ituraeorum sagittaria, II Flavia Commagenorum sagittariorum*. One archer of the third variety, dressed as a common auxiliary, is likely to have belonged to *cohors I sagittariorum milliaria*, or perhaps to the *I Cretum sagittariorum*.

58, 64, 109 The slingers are without cuirass, wearing an ample, but short tunic; in a cloth purse, hanging in front, they carry their projectiles *(glandes)*.

26 The infantrymen and the horsemen in auxiliary cohorts and *alae*, when lacking the above ethnic and/or specialized features, wear either a leather corslet or a tunic (simple or double); more rarely they are clad in a scale or chain cuirass. They always wear knee-breeches and sandals *(caligae)*.

Very often the auxiliaries wear a scarf *(focale)* and a cloak *129* (sometimes fringed). Their helmet is the same as that of the legionaries and praetorians, crestless, except in one case. Some horsemen wear a lighter helmet without cheek-pieces. In another case, auxiliary foot-soldiers of this type are seen fighting without a helmet, whereas in yet another they wear, in place of the helmet, a bearskin like that of the standard-bearers and musicians.

The auxiliaries are armed with the *gladius*, but the disappearance of metal implements from the Column's reliefs makes it impossible to verify the presence of local weapons *(spatha, conti*, etc.).

The auxiliary bodyguards, i.e. the *cohortes*(?) and *alae singularium*, are identifiable first by the fact that they accompany the emperor in his journeying on land and sea, and secondly by their wearing of marching-dress, cloak and tunic, instead of cuirass. Their standards and shield-symbols also seem to mark them out (see below).

The commanders of auxiliary units are very rarely recognizable. At the outset of the First Dacian War a *symmachiarius* officer (prefect) may be indicated by a figure, wearing a tunic and bearing an oval shield with a single star-like symbol, at the side of the emperor. In other scenes, not far off, two auxiliary officers stand behind Trajan as members of his staff. *10, 14*

Symmachiarii

On Trajan's Column the semi-regular units incorporated in the *exercitus* enter history, making their first appearance in the imperial triumphal imagery and playing their part, at the side of the Roman and auxiliary *milites*, in this magnificent sculptural commemoration. The 'cliché' by which their identification is made precise is that of showing them stripped to the waist and wearing long trousers rolled up to form a waistband; more *20* rarely they wear a short vest that leaves one shoulder ex- *31* posed.

They are barefoot, a detail of peculiar importance if one remembers that the condition of regular Roman soldiers such as legionaries and auxiliaries was colloquially described as *in caliga* (*in calceo* for the higher officers). It is easy to understand why the *symmachiarii*, as irregular troops without either the Roman citizenship or the right to achieve it, should have been represented as the only fighting men in the imperial army who were not *in caliga*.

Their weapon, when preserved (so often spears or swords are lost), is a heavy and knotted wooden club *(clava, fustis)*, typically 'barbarian', underlining the preservation by such units of their own tribal weapons. Tacitus (*Germ.*, 45) records that the German tribe of the *Aestii* (from what is now Estonia) were accustomed to fight with a club. But the only *symmachiarii* of whom epigraphic evidence exists in connection with the Dacian wars are *Astures*.

Furthermore, these *symmachiarii* have the long rough hair and beards with which barbarians are generally depicted in Roman art. They sometimes hold oval shields, but never the tile-shaped *scutum* or the *gladius* – further emphasizing the un-Romanized and irregular character of the way in which they served in the Roman *exercitus*. Their commanders are not clearly indicated, apart from the one already mentioned, and in this case it is uncertain whether he belongs to the *auxilia* or to the *symmachiarii*.

Among the semi-regular units represented on the Column, the Mauretanian cavalry also holds an important position, since it was led by Lusius Quietus, at the time a friend of the emperor and mentioned by Dio Cassius. The Mauretanian 54-5 riders can be easily recognized in one scene as a body of light cavalry, with unsaddled horses guided by a simple halter round the neck. The men wear a short tunic with a waistband of crude rope; their corkscrew curls are uncovered and they are barefoot. Their weapons are lost, but were probably short spears, and they bear a small round buckler *(cetra)*. The personified province of Mauretania is depicted with precisely the same characteristics and arms on coin-reverses of Hadrian (M. & S. 856, 858). Other irregular horsemen, without cuirass and hel- 24 met, are seen raiding enemy territory and setting a village on fire, but their identification is uncertain.

Finally, all the standard-bearers and musicians *(signiferi* and *aeneatores)*, when represented on the Column apart from their legionary, praetorian or auxiliary associates, wear the bearskin hood *(pellis)* that covers the head and shoulders, and a corslet, and have a round buckler *(parma)*. When they are in light marching-dress the *pellis* is not worn.

CLASSIARII

The 'cliché' of *classiarii* is not as definite as the foregoing ones and seems to rely upon the use of the axe, with a view to recalling the specialized 'axe-masters' peculiar to the fleet. *81*

Classiarii should, then, be identified as men with a short, draped tunic and wearing the *caligae* (sandals), who are intent on technical occupations and display their axes. In one case two soldiers, in legionary-praetorian armour, are fighting with the axe (see below). The appearance of 'naval crowns' *(coronae* *87* *navales)* upon some standards may point to the presence of *centuriae classicae* (a type of marine).

Naturally the crews (*gubernatores*, rowers, etc.) of ships and barges, which are often also loaded with land-troops, belong to the navy. A group of shipbuilders in legionary armour, busily at work close to a river, should also be regarded as part of the navy.

Military standards

The military standards represented on the Column's frieze fall into the well-known categories already outlined and are: legionary eagles, *signa, vexilla, imagines.*

LEGIONARY EAGLE

The common type shows a spread-eagle perched on a pedestal, *43* which is wider at the top than at the bottom. It is noteworthy that the emblem of the thunderbolt as a perch for the eagle is absent on the Column, while it is almost always on Trajanic coin-reverses of the time. The same distinction is true of the shaft, which is unadorned on the Column, but bears different ornaments on the coin-reverses. No exact identification of legions seems to be possible through their eagles, since no numerals are visible on them. Fröhner (in Cichorius) has suggested that when a pedestal lacks an eagle, there is an allusion to the disgraceful loss of an eagle by a legion. Such a case could be the *legio XXI Rapax* whose disbanding (by *missio ignominiosa*) might have occurred during the Dacian wars. All this is, however, highly questionable (Petersen; Paribeni, p. 225), for the absence of an *aquila* from its pedestal is much more likely to be due simply to damage. Anyhow, whenever the eagle is seen, it should symbolically indicate the presence of an entire legion.

Signa

The *signa*, as previously stated, are of two distinct types: praetorian *signa*, up the shaft of which are superimposed wreaths *(coronae)* and imperial images; legionary (and auxiliary?) *signa*, up the shaft of which there is a series of superimposed *paterae* (discs with concentric circles). Sometimes there is only one wreath and a crescent. A cross-bar, with two elaborate pendants, is occasionally inserted between the two uppermost elements.

When one compares the *signa* on the Trajanic coinage relating to the Dacian wars with those shown on the Column, one realizes that those of a 'mixed' type occur. Such *signa* have a reduced number of superimposed elements, probably because of the limited surface of the coin-reverse. At the top of the *signa* there is, generally, a vertical wreath in the centre of which is an oval shield, or more rarely the open *manus*, surmounted by a spearhead. Occasionally the emblem at the apex is covered by a *vexillum*.

The praetorian *signa* have been identified on the Column by strict analogy with those on other reliefs that certainly depict praetorian cohorts [for coin reverses, see Rossi, 1967(b)]; and they do not appear to have been substantially modified for conventional purposes.

Conventional, by contrast, seem to be the legionary *signa*, which are somewhat different from those represented elsewhere (on coins) and actually in use, especially as regards the higher number (4–5) and the uniformity of the *paterae*.

Finally, the auxiliary *signa* are indistinguishable from the legionary ones, provided one accepts the criteria suggested by the author in respect of later representations on coin-reverses of Hadrian and Antoninus and on the Column of Marcus Aurelius. In one case, however, a standard formerly attributed to praetorians (Richmond, 1935, p. 38) in fact belonged to an auxiliary unit; indeed its bearer displays a round buckler adorned with a wreath-emblem, identical with that of an auxiliary infantryman standing nearby. This standard, as well as another at its side, shows very few elements along the stem (two crowns and one patera only) in contrast to the usual legionary and praetorian *signa* on the Column.

It has been emphasized (Durry) that, on the Column, there is a regular grouping in 'threes' of the praetorian *signa*, which would appear to indicate that each *signum* belongs to a maniple and that the group represents the whole praetorian cohort. The emblem of the maniples should probably be identified, however, with the open hand *(manus)*, which is much more frequently seen on legionary standards, where it is shown in a pair, one on each side of the eagle, or above the emblem of 'wreath and shield'. These emblems of wreath-shield and wreath-hand at the apex are so different from each other that it is difficult to attribute both of them to the maniple. It is much easier to assume that one belongs to the cohort (wreath-shield) and the other to the maniple (wreath-hand).

In the case of a praetorian cohort the interpretation of a group of three *signa* as connected with the maniple may be correct, while in the case of a legion, the two wreaths at the eagle's sides, one for each cohort, may represent the *primi ordines*, i.e. the 1st and 2nd cohorts. Moreover, in one scene *(adlocutio)* there are three praetorian standards whose emblem at the apex is covered by a *vexillum*; these may represent either   39 three *vexillationes* of a praetorian cohort or the emblems of the *turmae* of praetorian cavalry.

On examining the superimposed horizontal crowns up the shaft of the praetorian standards one can recognize the *coronae vallares*, with a design of ashlar-work, the *murales* with masonry and a small gate, and the *navales* with *rostra*.

VEXILLA

The *vexillum* consists of a square, tasselled flag hanging on a cross-bar at the top of a plain shaft. Sometimes smaller *vexilla*   96 are applied to the uppermost elements of *signa* of praetorian type.   39

Vexilla are represented in association with other legionary standards or in isolation as emblems of mounted units (see the *equites singulares*). But the *vexillum*, whether isolated or inserted on a *signum*, may indicate a 'detached' body of troops *(vexillatio)* as well as *turmae* of praetorian, legionary or auxiliary cavalry.   39, 96

IMAGINES

On the Column these seem to have been mostly renderings of emblems of the legion (sacred animals), but they are almost completely lost. The *imagines* were borne at the top of a shaft and rested on a pedestal similar to that of the legionary eagle, at the side of which they should frequently have been shown; but the only recognizable one is the ram, which identifies the *legio I Minervia*.

Emblems on the shields

TYPES OF EMBLEM

Of great variety and extraordinary interest are the emblems represented on the shields held by Roman soldiers in action or left on the ground in a row when the legionaries are working. Almost all the shields are deliberately oriented towards the onlooker, with a view to displaying their emblems as true 'badges' and so to facilitate the recognition of the units concerned. Here, as in the case of the *signa*, the original colours would have added important criteria for an exact identification of individual regiments.

The emblems on the shields (tile-shaped, rectangular or oval) can be subdivided into two main types, i.e. legionary-praetorian and auxiliary.

Fig. vi   The emblems on tile-shaped shields of legionaries and praetorians consist of a complicated series of variations on a basic motif (centred on the *umbo*): the thunderbolt with lateral zig-zag (arrow-headed) flashes of lightning and wings. These symbols, so often used in Roman mythological representation for indicating supreme power (see below), are almost always associated on the same shield, but they are oriented in various ways and differ in their details, and are sometimes accompanied by minor motifs (crescents, stars, etc.). Much rarer is another design, representing a laurel 'crown' or wreath (*corona* or *torques*?), with or without a ribbon below (the cohort's
Fig. vi, M, N   emblem) and with stars or crescents at the side. The soldiers who hold both types of shield (legionaries or praetorians) are identical. Unique are two legionary shields, lined up with
50   others on the ground, which do not show the above emblems,
Fig. vi, G   but simple symmetrical volutes of merely ornamental value.

Thus the shield-emblems enable the observer not only to identify the legionaries and praetorians more accurately, but also to recognize the different legions and cohorts which are taking part in individual events represented on the Column.

Figs. vii–ix   The devices on auxiliary oval shields are much more varied and complicated and only in some instances could one consider them as proper 'emblems' or 'badges', to which a special signifi-

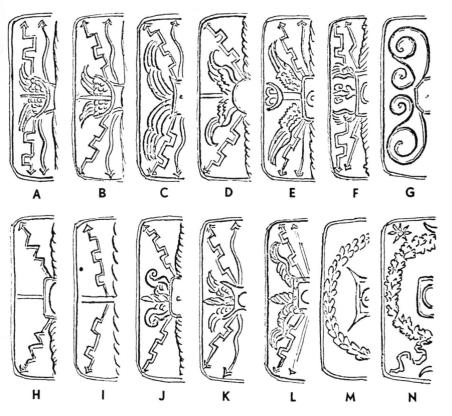

Fig. vi Legionary and praetorian shield-emblems. The symmetrical emblems and motifs adorning the front of the quadrangular shields (only one half of each is drawn) peculiar to the legionaries and praetorians on the Column.

cance may be attached. They mostly consist of symmetrical, elegant designs, rich in circles and volutes, of ornamental type and purpose.

The *leitmotif* of the 'thunderbolt-and-lightning', occasionally with wings and very similar to that on legionary-praetorian shields, is reproduced on auxiliary shields in a limited number of cases. Even rarer, but very interesting, is the representation on the upper half of the face of the shield of the Roman eagle perched on the emblem of the thunderbolt or on an arrow. In one case it is associated with the she-wolf and twins, shown at the bottom.

Fig. vii,
nos. 4–8

Fig. vii,
nos. 1–3

Fig. viii,
nos. 9–18
Fig. ix,
nos. 26–9

Fig. x,
nos. 31–5

Frequent also are the emblems of leaf-crowns or wreaths, single or double, centred on the *umbo* and associated with crescents and stars.

Upon the few shields borne by *symmachiarii* on which the emblem is visible, there are very simple motifs – a star with four to six points and two interlaced rings.

The Presumed Significance of Shield-Symbols

The emblem of 'thunderbolt-and-lightning', represented on the majority of the legionary-praetorian shields, can easily be interpreted, since it is commonly employed in Roman art as an 'official' sign of divine might (Jupiter), connected with imperial supreme authority and Roman power.

Fig. vii Auxiliary shield-emblems. The emblems and motifs adorning the front of the oval shields, countersigning the Roman auxiliaries on the Column (except for a few units *scutatae*): 1–3, units that were granted the Roman citizenship for valour; 4–8, units of Roman or Italian origin *voluntariorum civium Romanorum, ingenuorum* and/or *singulares imperatoris* (shield 8).

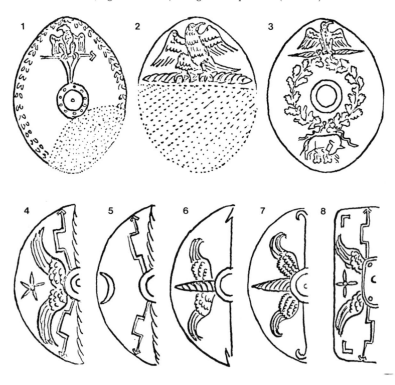

Fig. viii Auxiliary shield-emblems. 9–18, units with the title *torquata*.

In the military domain, as has been said, this emblem is often gripped by the claws of the legionary *aquila*. It is, moreover, represented on the shields of legionaries and praetorians in many reliefs (e.g. Louvre panel, Adamklissi's 'metopes') and on coin-reverses of Trajanic and other epochs.

Whenever this motif is present on auxiliary oval shields its symbolic value is, obviously, the same, namely to signify the might and divine strength of the Roman imperial army.

This emblem has also been interpreted (by Cichorius), in view of its ubiquity in legions and praetorian cohorts and its corresponding scarcity in auxiliary units, as the countersign of 'Roman citizenship'. Indeed, the original 'status' of Roman citizen belonged to all legionaries and praetorians, but only to a few auxiliaries (the aforementioned units *voluntariorum c.R.* and *ingenuorum*).

However, apart from the fact that the conventional 'cliché' for legionaries and praetorians on the Column in itself makes

the ownership of the Roman citizenship clear, the above interpretation does not, in the author's opinion, seem to be valid for
the following reasons: firstly some legionaries (or praetorians)
have shields with a different emblem (*corona* or *torques*);
secondly a better emblem for the idea of 'Roman citizen' would
be the eagle and she-wolf of Rome, a badge only found on the
shields of auxiliary soldiers, for whom the 'status' of Roman
citizen is the exception and not the rule. These symbols, moreover, are always absent from the shields of the *symmachiarii*, who
entirely lacked the privilege of obtaining the Roman citizenship.

It is important, also, to observe that an oval shield with the
'thunderbolt-and-lightning' symbol is held by a soldier of the
imperial escort in a famous Domitianic relief in Rome (Vatican,
see Toynbee). This *miles* seems to belong to the *singulares*, i.e. to
the auxiliaries of the imperial bodyguard.

Fig. vi, G   The only two legionary shields without any proper emblem
may belong to a unit which was deprived of its honours and
rights for disgraceful behaviour (cowardice, disloyalty); if one

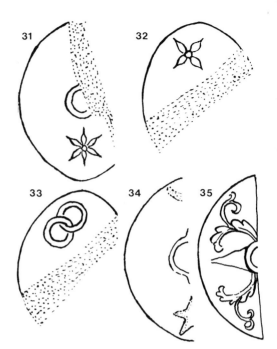

Fig. ix Left, auxiliary shield-emblems. 19–30, different motifs on oval shields of auxiliary units, among which the titles of *bis-torquata* or *torquata armillata* (27–9), and *cohors scutata* (the quadrangular shield 30) are hinted at.

Fig. x Right, 31–35, simple motifs on the shields of *symmachiarii*.

accepts the hypothesis that *legio XXI Rapax* might have been disbanded during the Trajanic Dacian wars, such shields could be attributed to it. The official, and sacred, symbols of the unit, erased elsewhere (as at Vindonissa), have been replaced by meaningless designs on the Column, since the legion suffered *damnatio memoriae*.

We should consider at this point the interesting possibility that some badges in the form of wreaths and leaf-crowns should be explained in the sense of *torques* instead of in that of *corona*. The two varieties of laurel wreath represented on legionary-praetorian shields seem actually to be *coronae* of the triumphal or civic type. This emblem is present on the shields of the first soldiers who, at the foot of the Column's frieze, are crossing the Danube, preceded by the eagle and standards of a legion, probably the *legio XXX Ulpia*. It is, indeed, a natural symbol of 'victory', which may be linked with the epithet of *Victrix*, bestowed upon the legion itself. The deliberate differentiation of the shield-emblem of these soldiers might have been intended as a compliment to Trajan, who created and named

31

this very *legio XXX Ulpia*. It has also been suggested [Rossi, 1966 (a)], in view of the fact that the shields of British auxiliaries are similar to, and associated with, the shields of that legion in one scene, that these auxiliaries, once they had gained the Roman citizenship, could be drafted into the *legio XXX Ulpia*, in which the incidence of legionaries from Britannia is the highest (Forni).

On the shields of *auxilia* there are also wreaths of leaves of various kinds, many of which are very similar to the festoons that are so often seen hanging on the sides of altars. It must be emphasized that such festoons, in Latin, are named *torques* (*nexis ornatae torquibus arae* in Virgil, *Georg.* 4, 276), a term which cannot but have a bearing on their military application. Moreover, the emblem at the apex of what is probably the cohort's *signum*, which consists of a kind of circular wreath, is sometimes described as *torques* (cf. Pauly-Wissowa, VI/2, p. 2450). On the other hand, it is usual to attribute to the military decoration of *torques* only the meaning of 'collar' or 'twisted collar'. Such an item is indeed sometimes present in the Roman army's iconography (see the famous relief of Varus' centurion, M. Caelius), but it is even more specifically represented as a barbarian (Celtic) attribute and ornament. On the Column's frieze such a *torques*, in the restrictive meaning of collar, is nowhere worn or displayed by the Romans, but is represented only on some Dacian shields.

The foregoing considerations which suggest the existence of a symbolic significance for auxiliary shield-badges can be further corroborated by the fact that the oval shields of the Dacians, while perfectly similar in shape to the auxiliary ones, show only ornamental designs and never exhibit figures of the emblematic type, either in the form of a wreath, or, of course, in that of eagle and thunderbolt. The only exception to this rule is that of a Dacian chieftain (a cap-wearer, *pilleatus*) who holds an oval shield with the latter emblem, a shield evidently captured from a Roman auxiliary unit.

ATTEMPT AT AN INTERPRETATION

In summing up the above arguments an attempt will be made to outline some criteria for the attribution of emblems and symbols to particular units of the Roman army. Attempts of this kind will be resumed later in examining in detail the reliefs

of the Column, in connection with various historical, topographical, and other data.

First of all, the emblems of thunderbolt-and-lightning (with
or without lateral wings), which are plainly pertinent to
legionaries and praetorians, when present in the context of the
auxilia should be considered as the emblems of *singulares* of the
imperial bodyguard (horsemen and perhaps infantry), as well
as of the *cohortes voluntariorum civium Romanorum* and *ingenuorum*.

This symbolism is, as has been said, to be attributed both to
the units which were originally 'Roman' and to those directly
attached to the emperor's person. Among the units which took
part in the Dacian wars we find, besides the aforementioned
legions and the 9th praetorian cohort, the following auxiliary
regiments: *ala I civium Romanorum* and *I praetoria singularium*;
cohors I campestris c.R., I Cisipadensium and *VIII voluntariorum c.R*;
the *pedites singulares Britannici*, probably also fall into this group.

For the other shield-badges, whose individuality and significance is much less clear, one has to try a series of hypotheses [cf.
Rossi, 1966 (b)], although many doubts will preclude any
definite conclusions.

The general criteria for interpretation are the usual ones,
supplied by some of the rules of Roman commemorative art. It
can also be argued that, in the interests of realism and of the
commemorative purpose of the Column, its authors and de-
signers selected as symbols of Trajan's *exercitus* the units which
were more closely linked with the emperor and more honoured
for their valour. It does not seem hazardous to postulate that,
amongst the chosen ones, there were the *alae* and *cohortes Ulpiae*,
to whom the imperial *cognomen* had been attributed not only in
reference to their recruitment, but mainly for distinguished
service in the Dacian campaigns.

As previously stated, the iconographic, as well as the epigraphical commemoration of the Trajanic wars was usually
centred upon the *miles*, or the unit, which had served Rome *pie
et fideliter*, earning glory for the 'republic'. These merits were
recognized by such honorific *cognomina* and *praemia* as the titles
of *pia fidelis, victrix* and *Ulpia*, and, for the *auxilia* alone, by those
of *torquata, bistorquata, armillata* (a very rare *cognomen* possessed by
the *ala Siliana* alone), and of *civium Romanorum*, in particular
when the citizenship was granted *ante emerita stipendia* for
distinguished service in the field.

If one were to compare the decorations and awards of the modern British army with those of the Roman, the titles of *Ulpia* and *pia fidelis* might correspond to that of 'Royal' bestowed on a regiment. The *torques* and the *cognomen* of *torquata* assigned to an entire unit, as to the *cohors I Brittonum*, is somewhat reminiscent of the wreath of immortals with which Queen Victoria decorated the colours of the 1st Battalion, 24th Foot (the South Wales Borderers) and which has appeared, from that time onwards, on the regimental colours and badge, in the same way as the *torques* on the cohort's *signum*. The abovementioned British regiment was granted the wreath for its valour at Roerkes Drift and Isandhlawana in the Zulu war (1879).

It is often impossible to ascertain whether single units had earned the distinctions in connection with the Dacian wars. But when this was certainly the case symbolic interpretation is always a possibility. We also know that Trajan was quite generous in distributing *dona* and *praemia militiae* during the campaigns; and the Column itself displays a ceremony of this *40–1* kind where Trajan, sitting on the *sella castrensis*, distributes gifts to auxiliary soldiers, who are bowing and kissing the generous hand of their emperor. It is also implicit that they had been granted the Roman citizenship, since the lack of it excluded the auxiliaries from the *donativa* (Cheesman, pp. 34, 35).

It is, then, possible to make a list, selected from the preceding one, of those units that probably enjoyed a preferential and conspicuous place on Trajan's Column.

(a) *Legio XXX Ulpia Victrix*
(b) *Auxilia*:
Alae: civium Romanorum; Siliana torquata (armillata) c.R.; Ulpia contariorum milliaria c.R.; I Flavia Augusta Britannica milliaria c.R. (bis torquata ob virtutem?); praetoria singularium. Cohorts: *I Breucorum milliaria c.R.; I Britannica milliaria c.R.; I Brittonum milliaria Ulpia torquata p.f.c.R.; IV Cypria c.R.; I Flavia Ulpia Hispanorum c.R.; I Hemesenorum sagittariorum c.R.; I Lepidiana c.R.; Ulpia Pannoniorum milliaria equitata c.R.; I montanorum c.R.; I Thracum c.R.; I Vindelicorum milliaria c.R.; III Dalmatarum milliaria equitata c.R.; I Hispanorum veterana equitata p.f.; II Britannica milliaria p.f.c.R.; Ulpia Traiana Cugernorum c.R.*

Moreover, it has to be remembered that the *legio I Minervia* received special iconographic attention probably because it was commanded by Hadrian, the future emperor, during the Second Dacian War. The legionaries marching under the standards of *legio I Minervia*, and preceded by the image of the ram, have the shield-emblem of type *C* (see Appendix C). *43*

The costume and the weapon also lead to a satisfactory identification of the presence of *cohors I Hemesenorum sagittariorum c.R.* among the oriental archers. The archer wearing the ordinary auxiliary dress should stand for the *cohors I sagittariorum milliaria*. *101*
20

In the examples just quoted the costumes and the standards may supply useful indications, whereas in the case of the many auxiliaries who are all dressed alike, without any ethnic or specialized features, the study of the shield-badges is the only means at our disposal for recognizing the indiviual units more exactly.

It has been stated that the idea of *Ulpia* and/or *pia fidelis* may be implicit in all the units elected to march on the Column's frieze and that the idea of inborn 'Romanity' is conveyed in the case of legionaries and praetorians by their own special armour and shield-emblem of the thunderbolt, in the case of auxiliary *ingenui* or *singulares* by these emblems alone.

We must now consider what symbolism is likely to have been chosen to convey the idea of *insignia honorum* and for military recognitions bestowed upon auxiliary units for distinguished service in the field, i.e. the title of *torquata* (and, perhaps, of *armillata*) and that of *civium Romanorum*.

The title of *torquata* would have been, in theory, rendered by the actual object (the Celtic necklace), just as it is on some military tombstones (as at Vindonissa). It has been said, however, that such a collar is more frequently shown as a barbarian attribute, and is therefore not likely to have been an ornament of Roman soldiers in a triumphal representation. This is the reason why the author believes that the emblem of *torques* has been 'translated' on the shields of Roman auxiliaries into the other object, for which the Latin language used the same term, i.e. the twisted 'wreath'. Such a motif had the advantage of conveying the very concept of the military decoration, together with an obvious hint at glory and reward, while avoiding any confusion with barbarian objects.

If so, the wreath-badges, so frequent on the auxiliary shields, would refer to *cohors* or *ala torquata* and, when double, to *bistorquata* (or *torquata armillata*, the bracelet being also a circular ornament). Again, the emblem of the title *civium Romanorum*, bestowed for merit on the unit, is no doubt to be seen in the *aquila*, with or without she-wolf and twins. Thus it becomes possible to pick out almost certainly from among the units mentioned the *cohors I Brittonum milliaria Ulpia torquata p.f.c.R.*; this is, indeed, the only one in possession of the complete series of titles satisfying the present criteria. Its badge, on the oval shield adorned with *torques*, eagle and she-wolf, denotes two

53 auxiliary soldiers (standing for the entire unit) in scenes which occur during the First Dacian War, and fit in nicely with the relevant epigraphical documentation.

The Porolissum Diploma (see p. 50) states that this cohort earned its *cognomina* and decorations during the First and Second Dacian Wars, and that the Roman citizenship had been granted in AD 106 to its British soldiers (and to Ulpius Novantico) 'pie et fideliter expeditione Dacica functis ante emerita stipendia' (who served loyally and bravely in the Dacian war, before their twenty-five years under arms had expired).

The available evidence is, of course, very slight for drawing definite conclusions in such a complicated and largely hypothetical field. Nevertheless, the above data alone seem to be valid for exploring an important and fascinating chapter of military history. Arguments of this kind will be further discussed in the course of the detailed 'reading' of the Column's marble scroll.

Summary

The above information will now be summarized in order to give a succinct picture of the composition and achievements of the Roman army on Trajan's Column.

(a) The *exercitus* consists of the following corps: legions, praetorian cohorts, their *vexillationes*, auxiliary *alae* (cavalry) and *cohortes* (infantry), *symmachiarii* (semi-regular troops), river and sea fleets with detachments of *classiarii* (marines).

(b) The proportion of auxiliaries and *symmachiarii* (non-Romans) is quite high, and this is in perfect agreement with the available data in written sources and epigraphy, as well as with the military demands of the Dacian campaigns. There are about twenty major battle-scenes represented on the Column. The auxiliaries take part in nineteen of them, the legionaries and/or praetorians are to be found in seven, while *auxilia* and *symmachiarii* fight alone in twelve. It becomes self-evident, therefore, that the prominent part played in actual fighting by the non-Roman soldiers serving with the Roman army has been recognized and commemorated with extreme objectivity.

(c) Again, out of eighteen scenes of field works and technical activities the legionaries and praetorians are the only troops represented in sixteen, the *classiarii* in two, the auxiliaries in none. Such a complete exclusion of non-Roman soldiers from technical achievements does not correspond to historical reality. It is most probable, for instance, that during the Dacian wars the *cohors III Brittonum* was working on the pillars of the great bridge of Drobetae, while it is beyond doubt (see Hadrian's *adlocutio* at Lambaesis) that the auxiliary troops usually built their own *castra, castella,* etc. The fact that on the Column all the technical and field work has been purposely attributed to the genuinely Roman *milites* carries a clear conventional meaning, aimed at a purposeful commemoration of the merit won by the intelligence and craftsmanship, as well as by the bravery, of the strictly Roman men and units of the army, and of the glory thus attained.

There is one very striking exception to this rule, which concerns the medical field-service, whose skills were carried out by auxiliaries. This reveals how greatly appreciated in imperial *36* times were the *medici* serving with the army, many of whom would have been, as was normal in this period, *peregrini* of Greek extraction and who could not, therefore, be depicted on the frieze otherwise than by the 'auxiliary' cliché. Another point of interest is raised by the official attitude towards the primitive, or barbaric custom, practised by the Romans and their foes alike, of beheading the enemy's prisoners and fallen. Beheading the enemy and displaying the gruesome trophy in front of houses and ramparts was a Celtic custom. The Column *20, 24, 50* admits that this grim practice obtained in the imperial army, but attributes it only to the *auxilia* (of Celtic origin?), never to the legionaries or praetorians, as though to suggest a difference in behaviour between the strictly Roman and the non-Roman components of the Roman army where uncivilized actions of this kind were concerned. This implies that the true Roman citizen, even when at war, will avoid all unnecessary bloodshed and cruelty – an implication that is clearly borne out by those scenes in which the emperor is performing acts of mercy and peace while fierce fighting is going on around him. This is just the humanitarian mood that Pliny the Younger stresses in his *Panegyric on Trajan* (13, 3; 16, 1). Nevertheless, the severed head of Decebalus was paraded before the army on a tray and eventually sent to Rome!

147-8

On the whole, the synthesis of the Dacian wars as shown on the Column could not be a better or a more balanced one at military-historical level. The power and skill of Rome's *exercitus*, its heterogeneous components united under the leadership of the omnipresent emperor, its well-considered preparation and work, its diligent watching and gallant fighting cannot but culminate, the spectator feels, in final victory and fateful triumph. On this matchless 'trophy' the discipline and bravery of the whole imperial army are commemorated, while well-co-ordinated and manifold technical superiority is shown to be an exclusive virtue of the *miles Romanus*, in the strictest and most traditional sense of the term.

According to the typical and exclusively Roman concept of military glory, the 'mind' in 'exercise' of the *exercitus* is destined to predominate over the 'arm' in bravery and strength of every other 'army'. And the Column still proclaims in the superb language of marble symbols, as it did centuries ago, the military apotheosis of Roman civilization.

CHAPTER VI

THE DACIAN ARMY

Composition

The first point to notice is that on Trajan's Column the non-homogeneous ethnic composition of the Dacian army is emphasized by the representation of warriors with different clothing and arms. But here, as with the Roman army, a certain degree of conventionalism has been adopted to indicate clearly to the onlooker the general character of the Dacian fighters. It is beyond doubt, as is demonstrated by the Tropaeum at Adamklissi, that in reality the costumes of the Roxolan, Bastarnian and Sarmatian allies were (see Florescu) definitely different from those of the Dacians proper (Geto-Dacians), whereas on the Column a clear-cut distinction can only be made between the Dacians and the Roxolan-Sarmatians. Nevertheless, in a few peaceful scenes, such as that of the armistice at the end of the first war, and that of the consecration of Apollodorus' bridge over the Danube, one can distinguish the representatives of the peoples living in the Danubian area, related or allied to the Dacians, wearing their national costumes.

27, 33, 152

90–1

Arms and equipment

The typical Dacian warrior on the Column shows the following characteristics: long and coarse hair and beard: an ample tunic with slits at the sides, long creased trousers, sandals of various types, and a cloak, which is often fringed. A special mark is the cap of a somewhat 'Phrygian' design, which is worn only by personages of rank such as tribal chieftains and leaders of bands. These are called by Dio *Daci pilleati* (or *pileati*), whereas the capless rank and file are the *Daci comati*.

6, 32

The defensive armament consists of an oval shield, identical with that of Roman auxiliaries, but with ornamental designs of a general type clearly devoid of any emblematic significance.

Roman symbols (thunderbolt, *aquila, lupa, torques*) are nowhere represented except in the case of a Dacian *pilleatus*, who is holding a shield with the 'thunderbolt-and-lightning' device, either captured from a Roman auxiliary unit *(voluntariorum c.R.* or *singulares)* or belonging to a deserter. The Dacian infantrymen in no case wear iron helmets or cuirasses, a fact which seems to confirm the view that representation of them is conventional. On the Column's pedestal, where the foe's arms are shown piled up *(congeries armorum)*, there are many helmets and suits of armour, some belonging to the Sarmato-Scythian cavalry, but others certainly to the Dacians themselves.

The offensive armament peculiar to the Dacian infantry is the *falx* (war-scythe) which is represented on the Column as being quite small and wielded with one hand, like a reversed scimitar, whereas in reality it was a large weapon brandished with both hands, as can be seen on the 'metopes' of the Adamklissi Tropaeum. This weapon was very awe-inspiring and

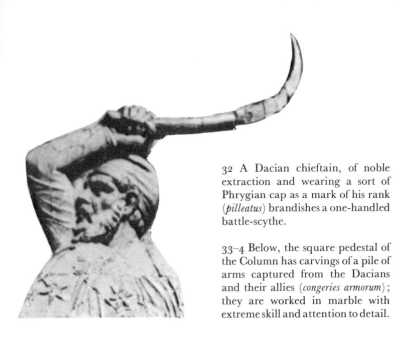

32 A Dacian chieftain, of noble extraction and wearing a sort of Phrygian cap as a mark of his rank (*pilleatus*) brandishes a one-handled battle-scythe.

33–4 Below, the square pedestal of the Column has carvings of a pile of arms captured from the Dacians and their allies (*congeries armorum*); they are worked in marble with extreme skill and attention to detail.

35 A peculiar sword-hilt, hanging from the belt of the scale-armour represented on the Column's pedestal. It is almost identical with that of a long-bladed sword of the La Tène type (*Fig. xi*, left) found in a Dacian hill-fort.

Fig. xi Sword found by C. Daicoviciu in a Dacian hill-fort.

unusual – a terrifying object when opposed to the short Roman dagger. Some foot- and horse-soldiers are, moreover, armed with swords and spears. The sword is of the typical La Tène shape: the specimen found at Piatra Rosie is thirty-five inches long with a handle of five inches and a straight blade less than two inches wide. There are numerous archers with a double-bent bow (oriental type), similar to that of the Roman auxiliaries. But the bow was probably also somewhat conventionally rendered. The actual weapon used by the Dacians would have been different, in certain cases at least; indeed, Trajan is represented in the act of examining a bow with curiosity (Richmond, 1935). The Dacians also used battle-axes (seen on the Column's pedestal) and wooden clubs.

Another important element peculiar to the Dacian army is the heavy Sarmatian cavalry, the famous *cataphracti* or *clibanarii*. These may be described as 'armoured cavalry', with both horse and rider clad in mail, which on the Column is rendered as a fantastic type of scale-armour totally covering, and fitting tightly to, the body of man and mount. The rider wears a *27,33* conical helmet and has his face unprotected, while the horse's head is covered with scales and has eye-guards. Such cataphract cavalry was a mighty instrument of war of Sarmatian and Parthian origin; and it was adopted by the Romans not much later than the time of the Dacian wars *(alae cataphractatae)*. In reality, the horse's armour was generally represented by a long caparison either of chain-mail or of hard leather scales, and the head was covered with a moulded plate. Such is the equipment shown in the drawings of Parthian armoured cavalrymen at Dura Europos (of a later epoch).

As offensive armament the Dacians used *ballistae* similar to *58* the Roman ones, and a ram-head *(aries)*, also of Roman type, *27* to break down the walls or gates of enemy fortresses. It must be borne in mind that correspondencies of this kind between Dacian and Roman armament (shields, *ballistae*, *aries*) could reflect the work of the Roman military technicians who had passed over to the Dacians either under the terms of the Domitianic armistice or as deserters from Roman units (see above). In one scene some 'Roman deserters' have been recognized among the Dacian warriors who are employing the ram-head to dismantle the wall of a Roman fort (Cichorius, II, p. 154).

As regards the weapons of the Dacians, the probable loss of metal spears, bows, swords and the like, which had been applied to the Column's reliefs, must be taken into account. As regards transport, the four-wheeled wagon is peculiar to the Dacians on the Column's reliefs and on the Adamklissi 'metopes'.

Standards

The exact identification of individual bands or units of Dacian troops, apart from the Sarmato-Scythian armoured cavalry described above, is practically impossible. Perhaps 'regiments' of a kind may be hinted at by the grouping of men under individual dragon-standards. These standards, which are peculiar to the Dacians, consist of snake-like 'dragons' with canine head and gaping fangs, probably made of cloth (red ?), sewn up in a sleeve-like shape, and fastened to the top of a pike to be inflated by the wind. Many such 'dragons' are represented on the Column's pedestal, in the pile of arms. Sometimes the Dacians hold *vexilla* (very similar to the Roman ones), which may be either their own or captured from the Romans.

Very few Dacian personalities can be precisely recognized on the Column. One is, of course, King Decebalus; and it is very probable that his sister and his sons are among the captured or slain.

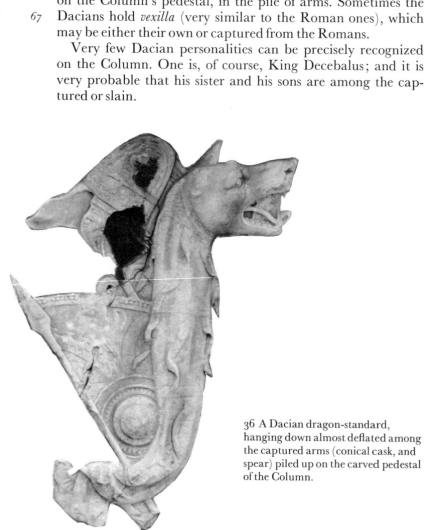

36 A Dacian dragon-standard, hanging down almost deflated among the captured arms (conical cask, and spear) piled up on the carved pedestal of the Column.

CHAPTER VII

RELIGIOUS AND MILITARY CEREMONIES ON THE COLUMN

Types of ceremony

Very many scenes show the Romans performing religious ceremonies, in which the emperor, wearing the toga, takes part as *pontifex maximus*. They mostly consist of the propitiatory rite of *lustratio*, widely practised in civil as well as in military *9, 47* *(lustratio exercitus)* contexts. Hogs, sheep and bulls are conducted to sacrifice *(suovetaurilia)*, while the emperor pours a libation of wine upon the fire burning on the altar.

The many *adlocutiones*, speeches of exhortation, edification, warning, or commemoration addressed by the emperor to his soldiers, while the staff and the standards of the units concerned are close at hand, are definitely military ceremonies. *39, 48* After important victories, the army gathers round the emperor, who stands with his staff on a platform; and the soldiers, raising their arms and cheering, acclaim anew their supreme *69, 124* leader as *imperator*.

On the other hand, Dacian religious ceremonies are not recognizable with certainty on the Column. It is, however, probable that the scene of the mass suicide of warriors by poison (at the moment of the fall of Sarmizegetusa) had a ritual significance. The Dacian chieftain *(pilleatus)* who is distribut- *118* ing the poisonous liquid, drawing it from a large pot, might be a high priest of Zamolxis. Again, the suppliant attitude of the Dacians, who are candidates for death, seems to suggest a religious invocation.

King Decebalus is also represented in the act of addressing the Dacian warriors. This last speech to his faithful surviving *137* soldiers, at the end of the second war, is again followed by a scene in which the Dacians are killing each other (with their daggers) so as to avoid falling into the hands of the encircling enemy. Soon afterwards Decebalus himself is surrounded by Roman cavalrymen and commits a 'ritual suicide', cutting his throat with a scythe. Finally, the famous scene of the Roman *41* captives tortured and slaughtered by Dacian women could be interpreted as representing ritual human sacrifice (C. and H. Daicoviciu, 1966).

Other military ceremonies, performed only on the Roman side, are those of the inspection of troops by the emperor and of their parading in front of him, either when setting out on cam- *19* paign or when approaching the enemy for battle. Both ceremonies could be regarded as true *decursiones*, whose importance in the Roman army from the psychological standpoint, was emphasized both on the coinage (e.g. Nero's *decursio* reverse-type) and on triumphal monuments (e.g. the base of the Antonine Column).

The presentation of prisoners to the emperor, acts of submission, and the arrival of deputations from the enemy are also to be classed among the official displays that culminated in the great scenes of general surrender, in the presence of the em- *66–7* peror and the army, at the conclusion of the First Dacian War. In each of these scenes the pose of the emperor has been carefully selected and repeated so as to convey the idea that Trajan himself was in active command of the whole situation and dominated everything and everybody there. Finally, even the straightforward scenes of Trajan's departure and arrival, unaccompanied by special ceremonies, have their own place in the sphere of imperial commemoration, a point demonstrated by the emphasis laid in the coinage on the motifs of *profectio* and *adventus Augusti*.

The gestures in imperial ceremonies

In connection with the ceremonies just described, some remarks may be made at this point on the subject of the meaning of the standard poses and attitudes in which the emperor is depicted – a theme which has been exhaustively reviewed in a recent study (Brilliant).

Firstly, there is Trajan's special pose in scenes of *adlocutio*: he is the only person gesturing, so as to emphasize his words, while his listeners stand intent and motionless. This is the case *48* when the audience is composed of disciplined Roman soldiers.

But when barbarians are present, they too gesticulate in a discourteous and disorderly way. On the other hand, when an *adlocutio* is combined with an imperial *salutatio* the soldiers respond to their leader by raising their arms in acclamation, as they do, for instance, in the scene of *imperator III* that comes just before the trophies at the end of the First Dacian War. 23

In every *adlocutio* the emperor's figure is oriented in the same direction: he stands on the left of the scene in a three-quarter view and faces towards the right. In other scenes, of either military *(decursio)* or religious *(lustratio)* content, where there is the need to stress the imperial authority and to emphasize the 'narrative' situation, the emperor's position is different: he faces towards the left and his outstretched right hand is open. In order to enhance this very gesture of implicit might, the right hand itself is sometimes of deliberately exaggerated size. 19 Combinations of these poses may be observed in scenes of the submission of vanquished enemies and captives. The group of Dacians, shown kneeling and unkempt in contrast to the clean-shaven and dignified figures of the Roman leaders, are raising their arms in supplication towards the standing figure of the emperor. Such a scene represents a kind of indirect bestowal of 128 power and glory on Trajan's image.

These various combinations of gestures and poses on the part of Romans and Dacians, in their appropriate settings, were intended to convey 'impact', that is, to evoke emotion by displaying the figure of the emperor in different situations – arrivals, departures, encounters, and so forth. This is often achieved 'iconographically', without putting Trajan in a specially dominant position.

To sum up, it has been confirmed once more by Brilliant's studies that on the Column, as on other imperial monuments, Trajan's achievements were allowed 'to speak for themselves' in conventional motifs in which significant moments of history were concentrated, and in patterns that were readily intelligible to the spectator. The narrative character and the realistic background of such motifs made it possible for them to be immediately assimilated by the public for whom they were intended and, we might add, to come alive again for the modern student after the passage of many centuries.

129

CHAPTER VIII

HISTORY IN PICTURES

Spirals I–XXIII: detailed description and interpretation

I shall now attempt to tell a coherent story of the Dacian wars by means of a series of 157 pictures of the marble scroll taken on the spot all round the Column, and of detailed photographs, either from casts or the original reliefs.

Each photograph of the series, which begins at the bottom of the Column, is identified by an illustration number; each reproduces one half of a spiral section, and thus comprises different scenes. For this reason, the individual scenes may often appear, in part or completely, in adjacent pictures. This should make reference easier and facilitate the weaving of the pictures into a continuous story. A Roman numeral indicates the beginning of each of the 23 sections, calculated perpendicularly from the starting point of the spiral, which is exactly above the mid-point of the dedicatory inscription. By counting the sections, the observer will be able to pick out quite easily both single scenes and entire episodes, at any point on the Column's frieze.

With the aid of all the information given above, we can now join, on the Column, the imperial army which is ready to cross the Danube and to open the operations of the First Dacian War.

The scroll begins with a sequence of pictures which are taken by an observer travelling up the Danube on a barge coming from the harbours of the Black Sea. He is facing, on the right bank of the river, the plains of the Roman province of Moesia Inferior. It is March in the year AD 101.

(I) The flat bank, beyond the wavy water, is protected by a regular series of block-houses and watch-towers, which are a local example of how the Roman *limes* throughout the Empire *1–2* was defended. The block-houses are ashlar-built, one-storeyed, covered by a gabled roof, and surrounded by a circular palisade of pointed stakes. They have a single window over a rectangular door, which faces the gap in the palisade that gives entrance to each. The watch-towers are also ashlar-built and hip-roofed, with two storeys. All round the upper floor runs a balcony with an upright railing and criss-cross slats; from the balcony's door there sticks out a long torch for signalling. These signal-towers *(burgi)* are also surrounded by a square palisade. In the spaces between the buildings there are flares of straw, piled up in tiers on a pole, for signalling by smoke, and tall beacons made of logs, for signalling by fire. Auxiliary soldiers stand in the foreground to represent the garrisoning and patrolling of the *limes* itself. Their shield-badges are damaged, but one is of recognizable *torques* type.

3

*Fig. viii,
nos. 14–18*

Spiral I

1

2

3

After this scene, which offers a concise and exact picture of the military defence of the frontier, we encounter the first

4–5 transport barges, with bows turned upwards to indicate that they have come from the lower course of the river. The barges are moored in small harbours on the Roman bank, with docks surrounded by palisades; stevedores are intent on loading and unloading barrels (first ship) and packs (second ship). This may well allude to the water transport of supplies for the Dacian expedition and to the storing of them in the open (in barrels) or in the docks of riverside towns.

Farther on the hills of Moesia Superior, where the expe-
4–5 ditionary forces were based, come in view. At the top of a hill
5–6 there is a partly walled town, entered by gateways crowned with crenellated towers. A third ship, loaded with barrels, is docked at the foot of the steep river-bank. The fortified part of the town covers a road along the latter. This fortified army-base is too close to the Danube to be Viminacium, and is more probably Pontes. Here our glimpse of the logistic preparation for the Dacian war ends; and from a cavern of the hilly bank
6 the torso of the personified Danube rises up to watch the Roman army's crossing upon two parallel bridges and its entrance into Dacia. Through one of the gates legionaries in marching-dress are leaving the town to step onto the first bridge of boats. These boats show the stern and the rudders clearly turned downwards, since they are facing upstream. Each boat carries, amidships, a stout pier of logs firmly held together by horizontal slats. In between every pair of boats there is a pontoon of closely fitted planks; and the piers and the pontoons carry the timber roadway structure of the bridge, with railings at the sides. Where the bridge reaches the Dacian bank it is supported by vertical struts. The legionaries are bare-headed, their helmets hanging from the right shoulder; on the
31 other shoulder they carry their kit (satchels, cooking pots and common kettle), fixed to a stake so as to be ready for in-spection.

The very first shields visible beyond the gateway bear the
Fig. vi, M 'crown' badge and are likely to belong to *legio XXX Ulpia*. The standards that precede the row of soldiers on the bridge are typical legionary ones, an *aquila* held by a bareheaded *aquilifer*, two manipular (or cohort) *signa* with simple *paterae* and a *vexillum*. An empty pedestal (for an *imago?*) is in the back-

132

4

5

6

31 ground. A high-ranking officer, wearing a double kilt, moulded cuirass, and ample cloak, leads the legion.

7   On the second bridge, which is to be thought of as upstream and is largely hidden by the first, a column of praetorian standard-bearers is marching, with several richly ornamented *signa*, one of which is partially covered by a superimposed *vexillum* (*vexillatio*, or praetorian cavalry). Trumpeters and dismounted cavalrymen in light uniform *(singulares)* precede the praetorians, while Trajan in 'hieratic' attitude, at the head of the guard, sets foot on Dacian territory. The emperor's figure has been planned to stand just above the dedicatory tablet and the doorway of the Column's pedestal at the end of the first section of the spiral. The motif of the emperor crossing a pontoon bridge at the head of his army to enter enemy territory is here specially related to the Roman celebration of *Virtus Augusti* (see coin reverse of Marcus Aurelius; M. & S.1047).

(II) The war is on. The Roman army, divided into two main bodies, penetrates Dacian territory across the bridges at Apus Fluvius (near the confluence of the Apus and the Danube) and Drobetae, respectively. The emperor marches with the body that landed at Apus Fluvius and so should have started from the base of Viminacium. He is escorted by the praetorian cohorts and *equites singulares* of the bodyguard. The 'emperor's own', *legio XXX Ulpia*, seems to have crossed, instead, at Pontes-Drobetae, with the other body of the army.

From here on the reliefs follow the advance of the section of the army under the personal command of Trajan (northern army), abandoning temporarily the other section (southern army). At Apus Fluvius the emperor immediately summons a

8   war-council; we can see him sitting on a platform surrounded by his staff, while other *equites singulares* with *vexilla* are leading their horses by the bridle toward the camp. Once the plans for invasion were settled, propitiatory ceremonies *(lustratio exer-*

9   *citus)* take place around the imperial *castra*, in the centre of which is the large tent of the *praetorium*, with three praetorian *signa* and three legionary *signa* (the eagle in the middle) beside it. A *vexillum* waves behind.

Along the walls of the *castra* an ox and a sheep are brought up for sacrifice. Inside, the emperor, togate as a *pontifex maximus*,

9   offers a *libatio* on an altar set up in front of the *praetorium* and the

7

Spiral II

8

9

standards. Afterwards, in the presence of Trajan standing upon a platform with two high-ranking officers, a barbarian falls from a mule to the ground in an odd attitude. From the mount's saddle a strange round object, riddled with holes, is hanging. This scene is commonly identified with an anecdote mentioned by Dio (LXVIII, 8, 1): an ambassador sent by the Buri (one of the Dacian peoples) carries to Trajan a message written upon a large mushroom's head, asking the emperor to withdraw. The action of this messenger, who jumps to the ground and gazes up towards Trajan, seems to be a traditional one among the Sarmatian peoples when in the presence of important personages (Paribeni).

At Apus Fluvius, Trajan is again on a platform between two 'generals', one of whom is wearing a corslet (a cavalry or auxiliary commander). The emperor delivers to the army his first *adlocutio*, which officially opens the Dacian war; and he is shown gesturing to emphasize his momentous words, while legionaries and auxiliaries, gathered around their standards, are listening intently.

The invasion of Dacia, emphatically marked by a large number of complex military works, begins with the building of defences, camps, forts, bridges and roads – a form of activity that is especially characteristic of the Roman army on campaign. It must be borne in mind that, on the Column, only legionaries, praetorians and *classiarii* are depicted as occupied with craftsmanship of this kind, while the auxiliaries watch and protect the works, without taking any actual part in them. On the left bank of the river Apus a *castellum* (fort) is under construction, connected by a bridge to a marching-camp on the right bank. Differences in the materials and techniques employed for such constructions led Davies to detect various types of camps (permanent *castra* and *castella* and temporary marching-camps) and the presence of the imperial *praetorium* within them. The working legionaries have placed their shields in a row on the ground. In the camp on the right bank, surrounded by a ditch *(vallum)*, Trajan stands with two officers, gazing northwards.

(III) The army is advancing along the right bank of the Apus and a circular marching-camp is shown, with legionary sentries posted before the *porta praetoria* and the *porta decumana*.

No Dacian resistance whatsoever has yet been encountered, and from this point Trajan, accompanied only by a *comes*, ascends a road protected with a railing towards an empty fortress at the top of the hill. At the foot of this hill a reconnoitring party of auxiliary infantry crosses a bridge, while a single soldier, a legionary, helmet-less and out of danger, is in the act of filling up a pot with river water. The site is probably that of Arcidava (Varadia), built and fortified on a hill-top, but lacking a water supply; and the soldier drawing water from the river below may be meant to suggest this situation, which was very important from the military standpoint.

The scene is, in general, a peaceful one, and the emperor, who walks calmly along and points towards a hill-fort, is obviously implying that the fort had been already evacuated by the enemy (Davies).

The next scene shows another small bridge and legionaries without helmets and shields, who are felling timber (road construction) out of danger, while Trajan's main force advances north-east and builds a camp, surrounded by a palisade and with the *praetorium* at its centre, at Centum Putei. Here the emperor inspects the works, having at his side two officers, probably prefects or tribunes, in auxiliary dress. Another small bridge is built and a group of auxiliary infantrymen, having crossed it, halts beside a new *castrum* (with central *praetorium*), whose gate is guarded by a legionary (or praetorian) sentry. Here, at Berzovia (Berzobis), Trajan with his *comites*, standing before the entrance to the camp, is confronted with the first Dacian prisoner of war, who is being rushed up by two auxiliaries, bound and held by the hair. It should be noted that the auxiliary reconnaissance and vanguard-parties are actually the only ones to make contact with the rear-skirmishers of the Dacian army, which had so far been retreating and avoiding battle. Farther on, at Aixis (or Azizis), two camps are being built on the opposite sides of the valley of the river Birzava, across which the legionaries are throwing a bridge with their helmets and shields at hand. Inside one of these camps the emperor is gazing intently upwards (north-east), having at his side, once more, an auxiliary or *symmachiarius* commander.

It is worth remembering that the itinerary of the Roman forces (northern army) during this part of the first Dacian campaign is fairly certain, since it has been recorded in the only

Spiral III

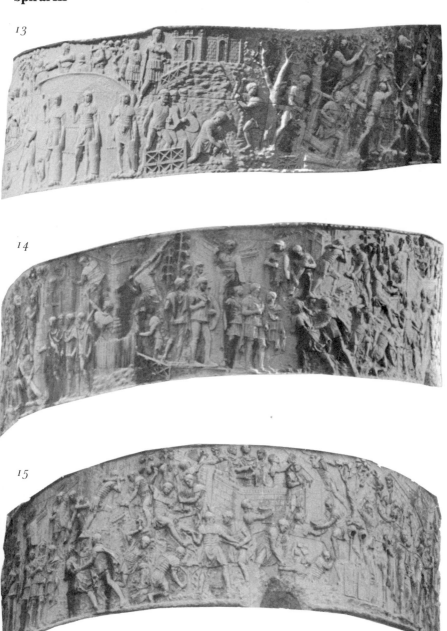

13

14

15

surviving line of Trajan's own war diary: '. . . inde Berzobim, deinde Aixim processimus'.

16   Soon afterwards, at Caput Bubali, a camp has been prepared and is guarded by legionary and auxiliary infantry, while
17   auxiliary cavalry crosses a bridge on the Poganis river and advances to the walls of Tibiscum (Caransebes). Here again the walls of the town are devoid of defenders; inside, houses of Dacian type are visible.

Near Tibiscum the northern and southern armies reunite. Legionaries, preceded by *signiferi* and an *aquilifer*, are shown marching obliquely among forest-trees from above downwards to join other legionaries defiling along the lower edge of the frieze and evidently coming from Tibiscum. Ahead, legionaries
17–18   are now felling trees to allow the passage of a road. The route followed by the southern army, in order to reach the region of Tibiscum, is likely to have been along the Mehadia valley and across the Teregova pass, on the ancient road ad Mediam-
Fig. iii   Praetorium-ad Pannonios-Gaganis-Masclunis. It is not known whether the southern force encountered any Dacian resistance on its route. It is probable that it did not, inasmuch as the detailed representation of Trajan's march seems to underline the complete lack of effective Dacian opposition throughout the whole of this first seasonal campaign. The Romans are energetically, but in a very orderly manner, engaged in organizing and reinforcing the logistic framework of the military occupation of Dacia. The Dacians, in their turn, have evidently resolved to avoid any encounter with the mighty Roman army on open ground and as long as their forces are divided. They therefore retreated in haste and gathered inside the hilly stronghold in the centre of which was Sarmizegetusa, protected by the Transylvanian Iron Gates on one side and by
Fig. ii   the 'fortified mountains' on the other. This afforded them a powerful defensive cover and deprived the Romans, in the meantime, of their superiority in strategy and tactics on a battlefield favourable to them.

(IV) The entire Roman expeditionary force, thus reunited
18–19   at the entrance to the Bistra valley, faces in force the Dacians, whose main body had hitherto been carrying out a strategic retreat. A violent pitched battle begins near Tapae (the Iron Gates of the Bistra valley). At least one legion and a unit of

16

17

Spiral IV

18

praetorians are drawn up as a rear-guard, while eight auxiliary cohorts (one of them *sagittaria*) and an undefined number of *alae* of cavalry attack the enemy.

Some *auxilia* display the severed heads of fallen Dacians to Trajan and his staff. Among the auxiliaries engaged in the front line can be distinguished irregular *symmachiarii*, naked at the waist and armed with clubs, probably Germans *(Aestii)*.

The Thunderer assists the Romans from heaven during a storm, aiming his thunderbolt (which was attached in metal and is therefore now lost) at the Dacians, who fight in full force, as is proved by their flags (two 'dragons' and a standard). The Dacians have to withdraw, apparently in an orderly fashion, for they are seen carrying their wounded through a thick wood. The battle is won by the Romans, who enter the Bistra valley where they are nevertheless halted at once by the Dacian fortified barrage.

20

21

We can then see Trajan standing with a high-ranking officer behind him; he is holding in his hand and observing a long arrow and an object (now lost), probably a Dacian bow. Below him, groups of auxiliaries set fire to a settlement with huts on piles, while in front of the Romans rises the wall of the enemy fortress, within which some retreating Dacians are taking refuge.

Inside the walls, which are grimly decorated with skulls on high stakes (those of the Romans who had fallen in the battle under Domitian several years before ?), one can see wooden buildings, a fluttering dragon and a *vexillum* (captured ?).

Before the walls, in the place where Trajan stands, are disposed some obstacles of the 'wolf-mouth' type, that is, a hole with a sharpened pole pointing upwards.

These powerful fortifications, obviously built with technical skill (perhaps by Roman military engineers in Decebalus' service), covered Sarmizegetusa on the western side and were sufficient to stop the Roman advance. In fact, immediately after this the scene changes into one showing two columns of

legionaries, without helmets (therefore, far from the enemy), marching through a wood. They then ford a river with their

equipment and luggage packed on their shields, which they

Fig. vi carry on their heads. The emblem on all their shields is of type *J* indicating that we are dealing with one legion or with a *vexillatio* of a legion. They probably represent the important reinforcements that are joining the imperial *exercitus* to replace the losses suffered in the battle at Tapae. Trajan, standing on a platform before the camp and surrounded by standard-bearers, receives an embassy of barbarians, on foot and on horseback (one of them has a shield), in the attitude of persons making a bold request; they are *comati* Dacians (bareheaded and with long hair), and therefore belonging to the inferior class and ranks.

(V) In the following scene, we can again see a Dacian

embassy; this time it is composed of elderly people, in a more humble attitude, but still belonging to the class of the *comati* and therefore possessing little or no authority or prestige.

In the meantime, the first great seasonal campaign (the first campaign of the First Dacian War) is nearly concluded with the pillaging of the occupied territory by the Romans.

22

23

Spiral V

24

25

On the ridge of the mountains some riders, bearded and without helmets (Syrian auxiliary riders), are galloping and
_{24–5} setting fire to wooden buildings, before which pikes with skulls are planted in the earth. On the plain, auxiliary cohorts raid the countryside and slaughter men and herds in the villages, from which the surviving inhabitants flee. Many prisoners are evidently captured. Indeed, in the upper part and at the
25 centre of this picture we find Trajan, accompanied by an officer, assisting at the embarkation (on long river-boats with the prow turned westwards) of a group of Dacian women, watched by auxiliaries. The emperor stretches out his arm towards one of these women, who is richly dressed and holds a child in her arms. She stands apart from the group and the presence of the emperor underlines her importance; almost certainly the sister of King Decebalus, captured by Laberius Maximus (Dio, LXVIII, 9, 4), she is in process of being transferred by way of the river Savus to the interior of the Roman territory, eventually to Italy.

25–6 The summer-autumn campaign is over and the following scene clearly moves to another field where, in winter time, a large contingent of Dacian cavalry, with the fluttering 'dragon', is crossing a river (frozen?) or a marshland, faced with great difficulties. Some riders are in danger of being swallowed up by the waters and are being helped by their comrades who have
26 reached dry ground (or an ice-field or sand-bank). Neverthe-

26

27

28

less, the passage seems to be accomplished successfully, since a
group of cuirassed riders, the Roxolan *cataphractati*, is seen
galloping on the other side of the waters towards the scene of a
big attack by the Dacian infantry on a Roman fortress. This
latter is defended by auxiliaries, whose shields show different
emblems. The scene, then, represents in 'shorthand' the assault
by the Dacians on a number of *castella* garrisoned by at least
eight cohorts of *auxilia*, among which there were a *cohors milliaria*
(two soldiers hold identical shields) and two cohorts *voluntariorum c.R.* There are many archers among the Dacian attackers,
and bearded men can be observed manoeuvring a battering-
ram *(aries)* of Roman type. This seems to imply the use by the
besiegers of siege techniques learned from the Romans and
even, perhaps, the presence of Roman deserters.

These last two scenes have been interpreted as the crossing
of the frozen Danube in a tract of its lower course (flat banks)
by the Dacians, who are making a diversionary attack in force
on the Roman garrisons of the province of Lower Moesia,
perhaps in the Novae-Oescus area, that is, far away from the
battleground in which the main body of the Roman army is
concentrated. The news of an impending danger of invasion of
Roman territory on the other side of the Danube forces Trajan
to embark rapidly with his *singulares*, horses and luggage on
cargo boats and warships *(biremes)*, so as to reach the threatened
area quickly. It has been suggested that the port of embarkation was one of the Roman bases on the middle course of the
Danube or of the Savus, or an Italian port.

The port seems to be of some importance, since it contains an
amphitheatre and an arch surmounted by a *quadriga*. It was
probably a maritime port in view of the presence of large
liburnae and of the fact that, were the ships descending the
Danube, the direction of their prows would have been the
opposite of the one represented (that is towards the bottom
instead of towards the top of the spiral). One should bear in
mind, however, that in its lower course the Danube flows eastwards (even north-eastwards). Hence an upward direction of
the ships' prows on the Column's spiral could have been used to
indicate activities on this sector of the river.

(VI) The emperor lands near a large fortified centre and
sets off on horseback at the head of a large 'flying' column of

*Fig. vii,
nos. 4, 5,
ix, nos. 20,
26, 28*
*Fig. ix,
no. 26*
*Fig. vii,
nos. 4, 5*
27–8

Fig. iii

28–30
*Fig. vii,
nos. 5, 8*

31

29

30

Spiral VI

31

149

auxiliaries; conspicuous among these are the German *symma-chiarii* armed with clubs *(Aestii)* and a 'regular' cohort (Germans?) whose shields are adorned with a *torques* and whose members wear a bearskin head-dress similar to that of the *signiferi*. A column of dismounted riders (a *cohors equitata* ?) is marching parallel to the 'flying' column. In a woody district the emperor meets other Roman riders of at least two *alae*, one of which is *civium Romanorum*, previously sent ahead for reconnaissance and now reporting that the enemy is in the vicinity. The auxiliary *alae* attack the cataphract Roxolan cavalry, which actually represents the bulk of the mounted Dacian troops engaged in this campaign, and put it to flight. The presence of the cuirassed Roxolan riders in this battle, and the importance of the victory obtained by the auxiliary Roman cavalry, seem to be indicated by the great number of weapons and pieces of armour of Sarmato-Scythian type which are represented in the *congeries armorum* on the Column's pedestal.

Next, the same cohorts of *auxilia* and the *symmachiarii*, together with cavalry *alae*, are surrounding and slaughtering the Dacian infantry drawn up before some wagons, loaded with pottery and supplies, over which the 'dragon' banner is waving. The battle is joined during a cloudy night which is hinted at by the veiled bust of the personified Selene (the moon) dominating the scene. Among the *auxilia* is perhaps seen the *cohors II Hispanorum Cyrenaica scutata*, represented by an auxiliary infantryman seen from behind, who is marching into battle and holding a tile-shaped *scutum* with legionary-praetorian features.

The place at which this fight among the wagons takes place is generally located in Lower Moesia, that is in Roman territory on the right bank of the Danube. The Dacian wagons are regarded as being loaded with booty *(amphorae)*, plundered during a raid into the Roman province. Nevertheless, it should be noted that the similar battle-scene represented in the 'metopes' of the Adamklissi Tropaeum ('metopes' XL–XLIII, see p. 63) shows the same wagons full of women and children, who are slaughtered along with the Dacian warriors. This scene might, therefore, represent not an 'incursion into Roman territory' by fast riding troops, who certainly would not have brought their families with them, but rather a sort of tribal 'transmigration' in southern Dacian territory, probably on the plains of Valachia and on the left bank of the lower Danube.

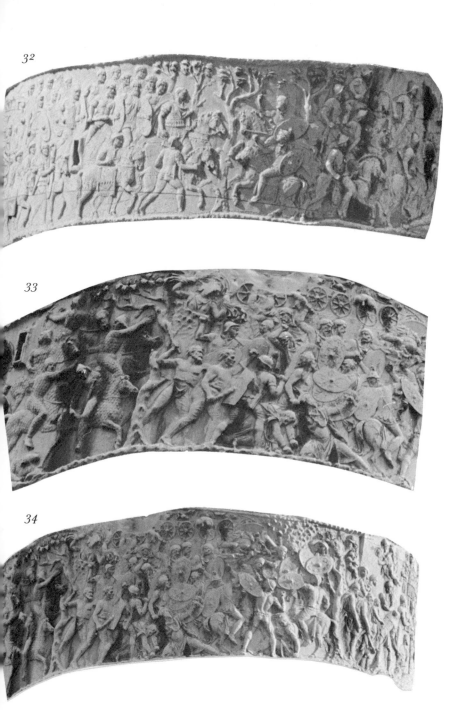

32

33

34

The next scene on the Column does, indeed, show men, women and children (an entire population) submitting and
35 asking for mercy from the Romans, who are intent on the construction of a camp, inside which Trajan stands with two officers. This scene recalls the military works that were usually put up in conquered enemy territory, rather than those of a province.

But the battle breaks out again, very fiercely, against a new formation of Dacian warriors. A pair of mules (drawing a
35–6 *carroballista*) follow two legions which take up their position
Fig. vi, J, K *(above)* with standards and a *vexillum* ready for the signal to be given by the *tubae*. Meanwhile *(below)*, the first prisoners are crowding up, amongst them a Dacian chieftain, *pilleatus*, wearing the Phrygian cap. There are also the Roman wounded,
36 who are receiving first-aid on the field from the surgeons of the military 'medical corps'.

Of the two wounded men one is a legionary (or praetorian) and the other an auxiliary (probably a cavalryman), hinting that both components of the army had alike shed their blood in the cause of victory. The legionary, in great distress, has been helped to the first-aid station by a comrade (or an orderly, *miles medicus*), and undergoes examination by a bearded *medicus*, who wears the complete auxiliary uniform and a somewhat elaborate light helmet. Meanwhile on the right, an auxiliary soldier with a wound in his calf is seated while his wound is being attended to by another member of the 'medical corps', who holds a roll of bandage and who is also dressed in the auxiliary fashion, but has a heavier and more usual type of helmet, and also looks younger.

It may be that in these two *medici* and in their activities the idea is conveyed both of the true *medicus ordinarius*, ageing, more expert, and of higher rank (note the elaborate helmet), who supervises the serious cases, and of the junior *capsarius*, deputed to use the *capsa* of bandages (the first-aid kit) and to dress slighter wounds (such as those of the limbs). The auxiliary 'cliché' applied to both is probably due to the fact that at this time the *medici* in the army were mostly *peregrini* without Roman citizenship, of Greek origin and training.

It is, therefore, important to emphasize that the medical field-service is the only technical activity shown on the Column that is entrusted to non-Romans (see p. 76); and that this

commemoration of its work represents a great tribute to its services.

It should also be recalled that Dio (LXVIII, 8, 2) records an episode in which Trajan tore his own cloak into strips in order to provide bandages when the supplies of these were exhausted owing to the great number of the wounded. This incident, however, referred to a battle at Tapae, whereas the fighting that we are dealing with on the frieze probably took place much farther south.

Fig. iii

This point may have a bearing on the question of the geographical transpositions in Dio's text that resulted from Xiphilinus' abridgement of the original. Another such transposition may have caused the placing of important funerary monuments at Tapae instead of at their actual site (Adamklissi in Moesia Inferior) (see p. 55).

36–7 The next scene of the frieze shows Trajan, with his general staff, standing before the assembled troops while a prisoner is being presented to him. The Roman mobile artillery, the *carroballista*, drawn by two mules and manoeuvred by a legionary squad *(contubernium)*, comes into action in support of the auxiliary cohorts and at least one legion that have engaged

37 the Dacians from different directions.

(VII) This battle-scene shows a large deployment of Roman foot units, with the support of the *carroballistae*, and of a small amount of cavalry, perhaps two *alae* only (one *c.R.*; for the

Fig. ix, shield-emblem of the rider above right); the action is directed
no. 27 by the emperor in person and results once more in the defeat of the Dacians who retire into the woods dragging their own

38 wounded with them. The pursuit is probably led by *cohortes equitatae*.

39 In the scene of *adlocutio* immediately following, Trajan addresses the *auxilia* (amongst whom are the *ala c.R.* and the

Fig. vii, no. 7 *cohors ingenuorum c.R.*) and the *symmachiarii*, all drawn up with their standards below the platform, to make clear that the successes of this part of the war have been attained through the *en masse* employment of the *auxilia*, while the legions were carrying out the tasks of covering, reinforcement, and fortification.

Within a 'concentration camp' guarded by legionary and

39–40 auxiliary sentries, we now see Dacian prisoners, many of them of high rank *(pilleati)*. They represent the fruit of victory; and Trajan, seated on the *sella castrensis*, is shown distributing

40 gifts and decorations to the brave soldiers who have been victorious.

Auxiliary soldiers are bowing before the emperor while they receive from his own hands their gifts (and, implicitly, the

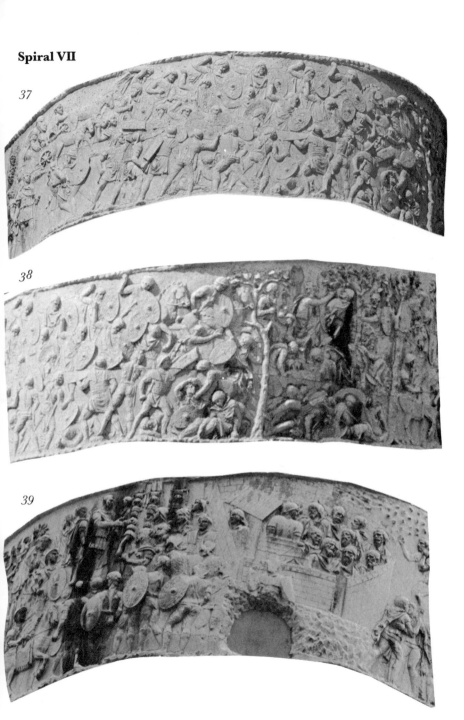

37

38

39

Roman citizenship); they then embrace and greet one another with joy.

At this point the scene shifts abruptly to a Dacian village, where the women are torturing some naked Roman prisoners *40–1* with pieces of iron and fire (a human sacrifice?). Joy and reward, pain and humiliation are intentionally contrasted to symbolize the changing and unstable fortunes of men at war. Again Trajan, wearing the toga, reappears outside the walls of *41* a harbour town to receive a new delegation of Dacian elders, who are in attitudes of submission and are accompanied by two auxiliaries. At the same time, a few soldiers with standards appear to have been landing with the emperor's suite. The town is situated on a hill: a *trireme* and a barge have their prows directed upwards. The place is probably a base on the Danube, reached by Trajan and his troops while going back upriver to central Dacia. In the following scene we seem to have an indication that this town is Pontes, in that from one of its gates a *42* legion emerges to cross a large bridge of boats, similar to the *6* first one represented on the Column. The legion is clearly *Fig. vi, C* identifiable as the *I Minervia* from the image of a ram, held by the *imaginifer* who leads the formation, near the legate and followed by the *aquilifer*. The *legio I Minervia*, coming from Upper Germany, crosses the Danube, together with the ex- *42–4* peditionary force, sub-divided into two or three parallel columns.

(VIII) At a lower level there are dismounted riders *(cohortes equitatae)*; and above (on the other side of a wall) legionaries, wagons and laden mules. To this army belongs, perhaps, the *legio XXX Ulpia*, which will appear later.

Fig. vi, N

It is the spring of the year AD 102 and the beginning of the third campaign of the First Dacian War. The march of the Roman columns does not, however, proceed in the same direction as in the preceding year. Having realized the impossibility of penetrating from the west through the mountainous belt around Sarmizegetusa, and confronted with the barrage of the Iron Gates of the Bistra valley, Trajan seems to have decided to attack from the east and south. For this purpose the army has to take a circuitous route, turning first eastwards at the foot of the Transylvanian Alps and then bending northwards, so as to pass up the valley of the Jiu and cross the Vulcan pass or, more probably, to pass up the valley of the Olt (Alutus) and cross the pass of Turnu Rosu.

Fig. iii

During this long march there are no important battles. Trajan, with his officers beside him, reaches a river and watches the legionaries as they step onto a small wooden bridge.

44–5

Having crossed it, the emperor halts at the camp while the legionaries are intent on operations in the woods (the opening of a road), and receives embassies of barbarian *comati*.

45–6

Things are moving. The emperor knows that hard trials are in prospect for the army and for this reason, wearing the toga of a *pontifex*, he performs the religious ceremony of *lustratio exercitus* inside the camp, in the presence of the standards. Outside the camp, sacrifices are taking place *(suovetaurilia)*, while the trumpets make music.

47

After this, standing on the platform, Trajan delivers an *adlocutio* to the troops. The legionaries, in a long line, resume their march towards the high valley of the Olt (or the Jiu) and carve out a road through the forest (among the shields lined up on the ground there is one without an emblem, see p. 108). Meanwhile, the auxiliary cavalry in the vanguard is raiding, and setting fire to, the villages evacuated by the enemy, who have fled leaving in front of their huts the usual impaled heads of fallen Romans. Trajan, riding with the vanguard, fords the river. In the background one can spot an islet that can be identified today in the higher course of the Olt. The walled building with a lateral gateway could be interpreted as a

48–9
50
Fig. vi, G
50–1

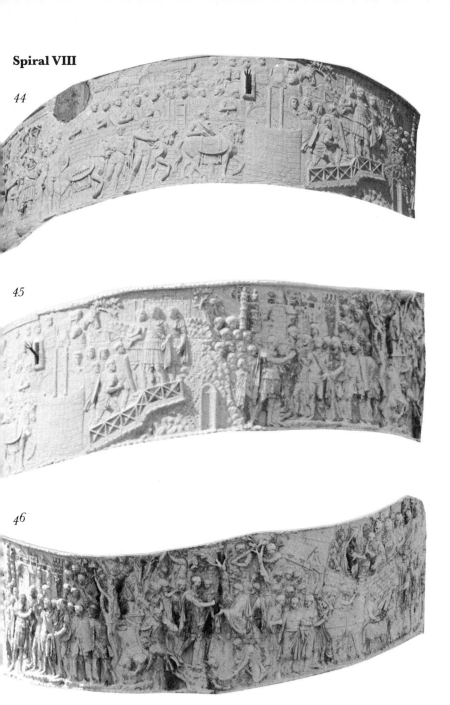

44

45

46

47

48

49

simple *mansio* and not as a proper fortification, according to the conventions adopted on the Roman maps (see p. 38).

Beyond the ridge of the mountains the main body of the Dacian army is retreating with its 'dragon' fluttering, while down in the valley the Roman auxiliaries are still burning out villages.   *51*

50

(IX) Now the army halts. The legionaries build two large camps, in one of which the wide imperial tent *(praetorium)* is conspicuous. Before the main gate, Trajan, with Sura and   *52* Livianus, receives the homage of a kneeling Dacian chieftain, a cap-wearer, who has been brought into his presence by a high-ranking Roman officer, followed by *tubicines* and *signiferi*.

It is recorded by Dio (LXVIII, 9, 1) that in this period of the war, Decebalus sent over to Trajan high-ranking messengers, who asked in vain for a personal audience with a view to obtaining a truce.

Trajan's army is now in hilly country in front of the western   *53* buttress of the fortified stronghold of the Dacians (Cibinului and Sebesului mountains). One can, in fact, see auxiliaries

51

from different cohorts and legionaries lined up at the foot of the hills on which other legionaries and praetorians are moving amid cylindrical, round-roofed buildings. These strange structures with no windows and arched gateways, flanked by tall trees (interpreted as cypresses), have been held to be the funerary monuments to which Dio Cassius refers (LXVIII, 8, 2). They would have been dedicated at Tapae to the fallen soldiers of the previous Dacian campaign. A recent suggestion is that Dio's *bomoi* (altars dedicated to the fallen) were originally mentioned in another passage (referring to Adamklissi) and have been erroneously attributed to Tapae only in Xiphilinus' epitome of Dio's history. On the Column they are evidently

Fig. iii much nearer to Tapae than to Adamklissi (see Baradez).

From the shield-emblems of the auxiliaries it is possible to

Fig. vii, no. 3 detect the presence of a *cohors torquata civium Romanorum*, which the author has assumed to be the *cohors I Brittonum milliaria Ulpia torquata p.f.c.R.* (see pp. 50–1). Among the legionaries there

Fig. vi, M is a shield adorned with a kind of *torques* wreath, directly facing that of the above-mentioned auxiliary unit and probably hinting at the *legio XXX Ulpia*.

After this, Trajan, standing on a rock in a dominant position,

54 watches a large body of galloping auxiliary horsemen, easily recognizable as the Moors of Lusius Quietus; they have curled hair, short tunics, no saddle and a single bridle, and are very similar, in their costume, to the personification of Mauretania on coin-reverses.

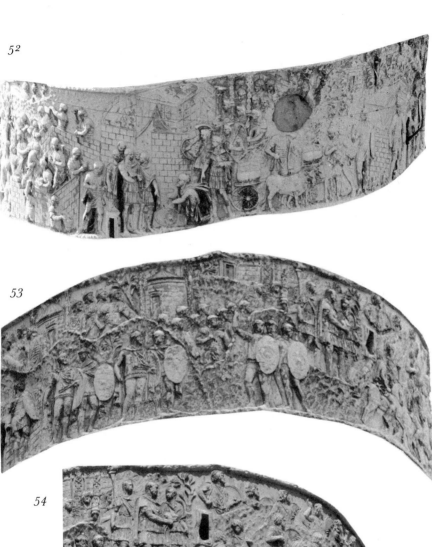

52

53

54

55

(X) The riders are probably swarming beyond the pass of Turnu Rosu, while the Dacians put up some resistance, before retiring into the forests. In the same forests are marching auxiliary cohorts, who encamp in a *castrum* built by the legionaries in front of a group of hills crowned with Dacian fortifications. Trajan and his general staff now superintend the preparation of a general attack on the strongholds: the *ballistae* are being brought up to be placed in strong pits lined with beams.

The presence of elaborate entrenchments, with 'artillery' in position and with a great legionary camp in the background, suggests that the Romans are preparing to besiege a Dacian citadel by establishing semi-permanent fortifications all round *(circumvallatio)* – so as to cover it with long-range weapons and prevent the enemy from either escaping or being reinforced. A comparable situation of this kind was that at Masada, the Zealot's fortress on the Dead Sea, which has recently provided the subject of a most detailed illustration of Roman siege-techniques (Yadin). The employment of these very techniques against Thracian hill-forts of the type we are dealing with is recorded by Tacitus (*Ann.* IV, 49), who states that Poppaeus Sabinus, while suppressing a revolt in Thracia (AD 26), sur-rounded a mountain stronghold with a long wall and ditch, reinforced by pits. Thus the water and crop supply of the be-sieged rebels was cut off; and they were kept under a con-tinuous fire of arrows (by the *sagittarii*), stones (by the *funditores*) and javelins by the Romans.

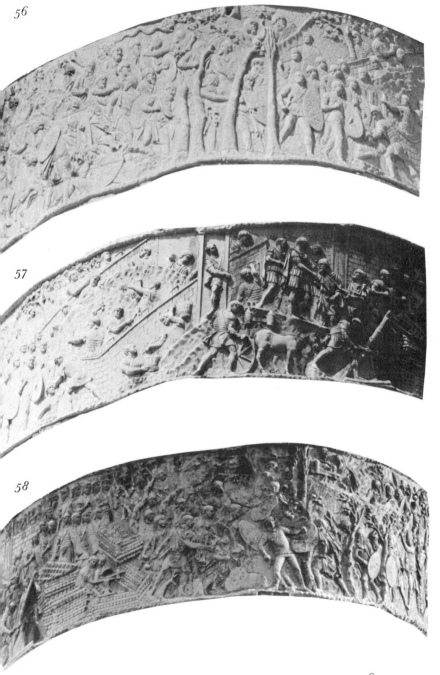

The problem of what the Dacian citadel might have been like has been tackled by examining *cetati* with remnants of Roman *castra* close by. The one fulfilling this condition (besides Sarmizegetusa) was Costesti, the hill-fort that blocked the access to the upper valley of the Apa Gradistei, protecting the approach to Sarmizegetusa from the north-west (see p. 222). It is therefore likely that the scene depicted on the Column shows the Romans' difficult task of dealing with the Dacian stronghold of Costesti. The first assault is carried out by different auxiliary infantry cohorts (one of which is *civium Romanorum*) with the support of at least one cohort of slingers and one of oriental troops (with conical helmet and *lorica squamata*). The fortress is defended by a palisade, upon which a *ballista* of Roman type, manipulated by the Dacians, is mounted. The Romans do not seem to be able to take the position.

Meanwhile, the Dacians busy themselves with felling trees to reinforce their defences. It is interesting to note that archaeology (C. Daicoviciu, 1954, p. 156) confirms that the Dacian forts on hilltops (e.g. Piatra Rosie; see below), originally built in stone *(murus gallicus)*, had been widened and reinforced in haste by adding palisades under the impending menace of the Roman attack. This is, moreover, clearly hinted at on the relief, which shows behind the Dacians, who are felling and cutting up trees in a great hurry, a square, stone structure with palisades on both sides, on a hill-crest.

The legionaries are also intent on similar works, but in an orderly and methodical fashion (their shields and helmets are on the ground); the auxiliaries stand on guard and round up prisoners, one of whom, a Dacian *pilleatus*, is brought before Trajan and his staff by two auxiliaries.

(XI) The Romans launch a renewed attack on a double hill-fort, whose peculiar features and identification will be discussed below. The assault is carried out by a strong detachment of auxiliary units, comprising regular infantry cohorts, flanked by a body of *symmachiarii* and by at least one cohort of specialized oriental archers and one of slingers. The auxiliary infantry and the *symmachiarii* (bare-chested, but presumably armed with spears), whose shield-emblem is a simple motif of star and crescent, are all drawn up in a single battle-line; the archers, clad in leather corslet with a long skirt underneath and

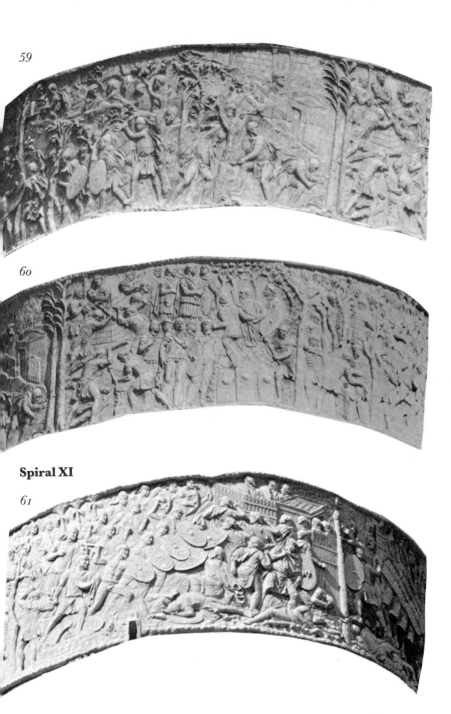

59

60

Spiral XI

61

wearing a conical helmet, are covering them at the rear, probably aiming their arrows at the defenders over the heads of the attackers. For the same purpose a unit of auxiliary slingers has joined in the battle. The Dacians are resisting valiantly and even attempt a sally, which, however, is repulsed by the Romans.

Let us now examine in detail the Dacian fort under attack, for it presents some characteristics which may suggest its location and provide a further proof of the generally realistic background of the Column's frieze.

First of all, it recalls the earlier representation of a Dacian 59 hill-fort, whose ramparts are being widened and reinforced, since it consists of a double structure of palisades and of masonry (probably *murus gallicus*).

In this case, however, it is clear that a long and angular (to hint at a quadrilateral outline) palisade forms a kind of enclosure, in which the stone-walled structure, with a lateral 61 turret, in the centre of which is a narrow gateway, lies on an apparently higher piece of ground. This type of fortress tallies with what has been found by the Rumanian archaeologists when excavating the ruins on the hill-top of Piatra Rosie.

There, at the very top, can be seen the original quadrangular stone-walled fort, whose gate opened through a corner-tower and led into an adjoining, much larger fort, surrounded by palisades, on the slope of the hill. Such a 'fortified mountain', as it appeared to the Roman assailants coming from the south and east, was an awe-inspiring sight.

Indeed, the frieze shows the Roman forces, drawn up for battle and approaching the long palisades, while the Dacians who had taken part in the sally are retreating hastily into the palisaded section of the stronghold and thence into the stone-walled fort. While they are entering the narrow gateway of the latter, it is probable that the auxiliary Roman cohorts, weakened by the fierce resistance of the Dacians, had already lost their momentum, so that one legion had to intervene to invest, with its own specially skilled siege-technique, the stone-walled fort at the hill-top. *62*

Here the representation on the Column is very precise. While the Dacians are gathering inside their last defences, the legionaries approach them with the famous *testudo*, a kind of turtle-shell, square formation produced by the soldiers' inter-locking quadrangular shields, which give the impression of a *Fig. vi, H* tiled roof and afford good protection as the soldiers come closer to the defended ramparts. The frieze also shows another interesting detail: the legionaries, drawn up in the *testudo*, are going up a slope on steps just like those of the staircase leading to the fort's gateway which the recent excavations at Piatra Rosie have revealed. Thus the peculiar features of the 'double fort' at Piatra Rosie seem to have been so clearly reproduced in the scene of the Roman assault that one could imagine it to be a skilful copy of an original cartoon drawn on the spot. More-over, this scene, with its vivid realism, would have been chosen for its power to evoke the memory and glory of the hectic attacks on the hill-top strongholds at the climax of the Dacian wars.

63

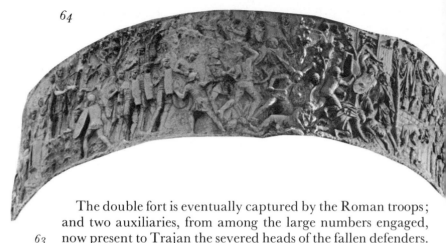

64

The double fort is eventually captured by the Roman troops; and two auxiliaries, from among the large numbers engaged, now present to Trajan the severed heads of the fallen defenders.

63
Fig. vi, D, N

At least two legions, one of which is the *XXX Ulpia*, are deployed in line of battle *(ordo)* to invest another fortress, either at Costesti or at Hulpe. The attack seems to involve great difficulty for the Romans, in spite of the use of the abovementioned legions.

64

A legionary is, indeed, represented in the act of turning his back to the enemy and retreating in haste without his shield (it was a great disgrace for a soldier to lose his shield). Once more a violent push by the *auxilia* seems to restore the critical situation.

Fig. viii,
no. 12

At least two infantry cohorts, clad in chain-mail cuirass, go into action covered by the slingers and the *symmachiarii*, one of which is seen fighting furiously ahead of the fleeing legionary. The Dacian defenders are overwhelmed in a fierce struggle before the palisades of their fortress. Here, perhaps, the *legio XXX Ulpia* may have won the title of *Victrix*. The legionaries are in fact building their *castrum* farther on, in the conquered hills; on its wall a shield with the crown of victory catches the eye.

65
Fig. vi, N

It is also possible that the fleeing legionary might represent the shocking behaviour of an entire unit (*legio XXI Rapax ?*), as has been suggested earlier.

Fig. vi, G

Inside this Roman camp Trajan discusses the important victory with his staff and addresses a group of soldiers and officers, probably praetorians, with crested helmets (and shield-emblem *E*). Meanwhile, legionaries are working at new defences nearby.

Fig. vi

The fall of the entire system of mountain-strongholds which protected Sarmizegetusa from the west and south opens to the Romans the approach to the Dacian capital. Decebalus probably must have realized, at this point, that there was no hope of restoring the military situation and so must have decided to ask the Roman emperor for an armistice and submitted to the conditions of a truce while planning a future revenge, instead of courting immediate and utter ruin.

Fig. iii

The Roman auxiliary cavalry and infantry, and probably also *cohortes equitatae*, are now watering at Aquae in complete security at a ford that flows from a thermal basin (with a plug at the bottom); legionaries in marching-dress and with shouldered packs are occupying a walled place that could well be Sarmizegetusa, in view of the fact that this picture merges into the great scene of the surrender of the Dacians, either in front of

Fig. viii, nos. 11–15
65

66

65

66

the walls of the capital or nearby. Trajan, seated on a platform *(suggestus)* and surrounded by the staff, the standards, and the troops (many of them auxiliaries), receives the surrender of kneeling Dacian chieftains *(pilleati)*, while Decebalus, at the rear (hinting at the order in which he and his chieftains asked for a truce) is also kneeling in an imploring attitude, with both arms raised towards the emperor.

A group of Dacians is standing with greater dignity (they are probably deputies destined to accompany Trajan to Rome) in front of another group of kneeling warriors whose shields are on the ground, while their arms are outstretched.

66–7

(XII) Farther on (also in the order in which they surrendered) another group of Dacian warriors is kneeling with outstretched arms in a suppliant attitude; just after this, however, the ground-line of the scene is interrupted by a rocky terrain, upon which there are many other Dacians, also in a suppliant attitude, but standing up and holding their standards and 'dragons' unfurled. Behind them, and looking over them, is Decebalus again, this time dressed as a commander and not as suppliant. The following scene reflects with great precision the hard conditions imposed by Trajan, known to us from historical sources. The Dacians must dismantle their fortresses (we can see some of them in the act of demolishing a stone wall, perhaps at Blidaru) and evacuate the hilly heart of their country; women, children and old people are seen coming down from the mountains. In the meantime, the same scene shows some Dacians whispering to one another in a conspiratorial way inside the walls of an intact fort, while in the mountain villages other barbarians are half-hidden from view and herds are to be seen. On the whole, the picture of the situation at the end of the First Dacian War, after the humiliating surrender, makes it clear that a strong contingent of warriors, led by Decebalus himself, has gained the mountains in defiance of the pacts, and that the armistice conditions imposed by the Romans are respected and carried out only in part (see Davies).

67–8

68

The strength of the Dacian army and its chief is still holding out, while many are conspiring and hiding so as not to fulfil the Roman demands. Thus it is clear that the situation is ripening for the outbreak of a new conflict. In the meantime, Trajan is delivering a peace *adlocutio* to his soldiers, who are in 'undress'

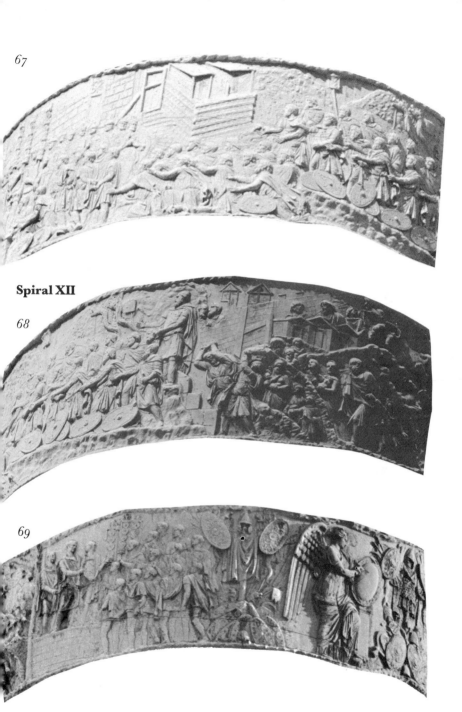

67

Spiral XII

68

69

69   uniform, wearing short tunics and carrying no arms. He is here
being proclaimed *imperator* by the army for the third time.

69–70   The figure of the winged Victory, inscribing a shield and
flanked by two trophies, officially concludes the history in
pictures of the First Dacian War.

Two years of peace follow, unrecorded on the Column's
reliefs, during which we know that the emperor was in Rome,
while in occupied Dacia the Romans consolidated their position, chiefly by means of such activities, of equal military and
civil importance, as the completion of the great bridge at

89   Drobetae and of an adequate road-system, protected by a network of *castra* and *castella*.

But in the meantime Decebalus strengthens the resistance
against Roman occupation and penetration. He obviously
realizes the danger of these very works (bridges, roads, forts),
which are already in an advanced stage and which will soon
allow the Romans to reach and dominate the country by
rapidly assembling and distributing troops and supplies.

The deteriorating situation in Dacia becomes evident to
Trajan, who decides to go there.

70–1   So the story in pictures starts again at Ancona, where Trajan,
who is wearing a heavy cloak (it is the winter of the year AD 105),
is escorted to the harbour by citizens holding torches (therefore
by night) and embarks hastily on ships of the Adriatic fleet,
accompanied by the praetorian guard and his suite. The town
of Ancona is identifiable from the fact that the port is situated
within a deep gulf (from which ships can go to sea), and also
from the acropolis, from the temple of Venus, and perhaps also

70   from an arch which occupies the position of Trajan's existing
arch in that city. This arch was not erected until AD 113, but
Apollodorus, the architect, had probably already designed it
at the time at which the Column's frieze was being carved.

(XIII) Trajan lands on the Dalmatian coast, where he is
72   warmly welcomed by the population and meets the local
72–3   authorities in the vicinity of a large square *porticus*, somewhat
reminiscent of the symbolic sketch for places named *Aquae* in
9, 73   Peutinger's Table. After this Trajan travels again by sea,
reaches another port, and on landing passes through a small
74   arch, to be received by joyful people and several children
(suggesting a Roman colony). Here great ceremonies are

70

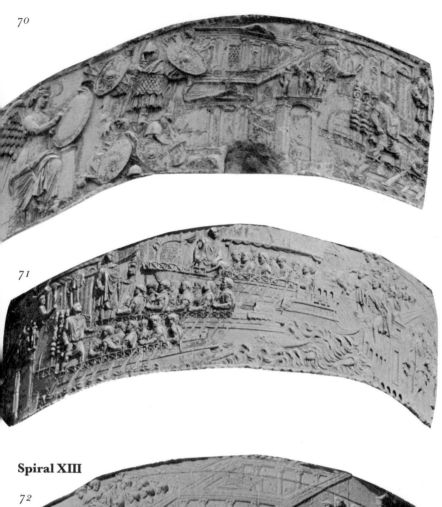

71

Spiral XIII

72

73

74

75   carried out, with the sacrifice of many oxen, while soldiers of
the garrison (or the escort) in 'undress' uniform and holding
standards are cheering. By sea again Trajan reaches a larger

76   town, with a theatre, a temple and other fine buildings
(variously interpreted as Corinth, Piraeus, Byzantium, or a
Dalmatian city), where he lands, stepping across a series of

Fig. vii, no. 4   arches (of an aqueduct?), followed by the *singulares* and their

76   *signa*. Another sacrifice of an ox and a libation are performed.

77   Then Trajan re-embarks, to go ashore at last at what is probably Salonae; riding fast, escorted always by his *equites singulares*

78–9   in travelling cloak and waving the *vexillum*, he reaches eventually an important centre of the interior, perhaps Sirmium in
Pannonia. It is of interest to note that throughout his journey

176

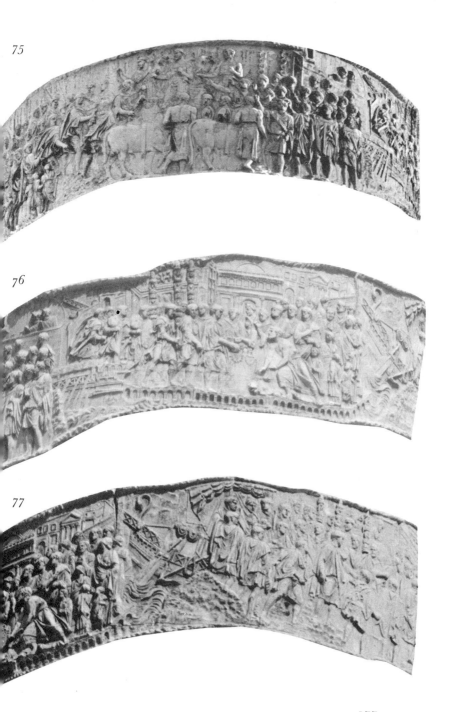

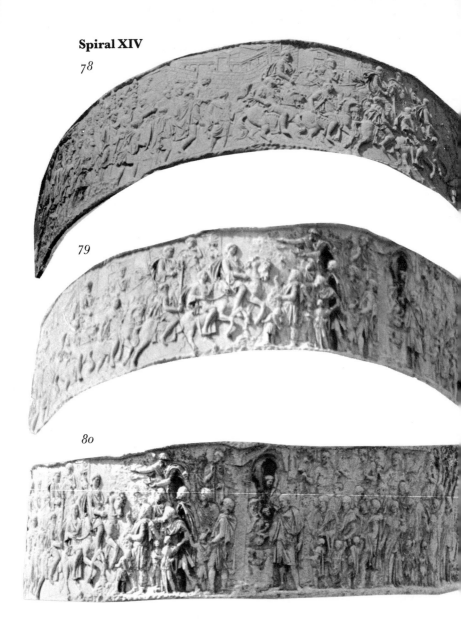

78

79

80

the emperor is heavily dressed, just like his military escort, from
79 which he is formally indistinguishable. This custom of Trajan,
who liked to travel without any pompous ostentation, was
praised in Pliny's *Panegyric on Trajan* (20, 3–4).

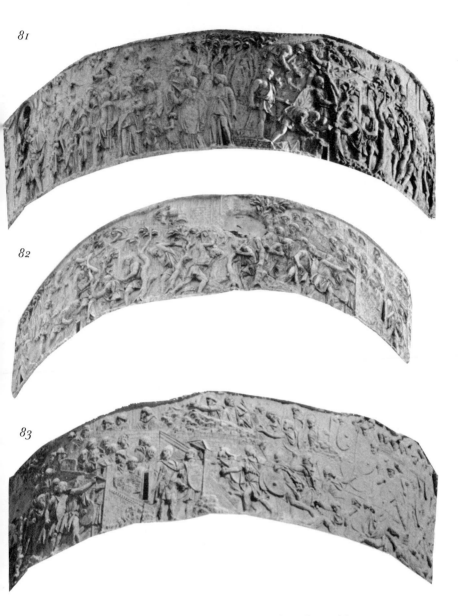

81

82

83

(XIV) Again Trajan is heartily welcomed and presides at a
great religious ceremony by pouring a libation upon an altar   *79–80*
before a small temple, in the presence of the population,
including women and children. In the background, sacrifices   *80–1*

179

84

85

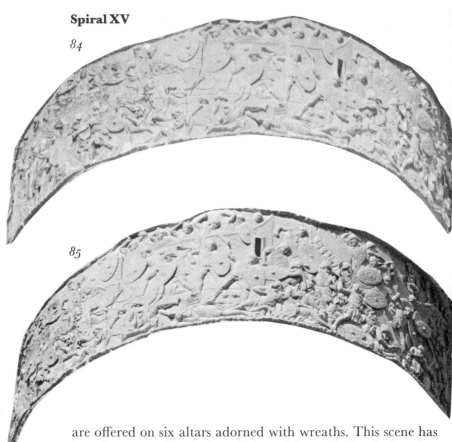

are offered on six altars adorned with wreaths. This scene has been interpreted as the foundation of Nicopolis; but its location at Tapae has also been suggested, which would imply a quite *Fig. i* different sea and land itinerary for Trajan. The direction of Trajan's movements, as they are represented on the spiral, and the presence of hexagonal shields of Germanic type (hanging on the trees) at the end of the scene, seem to support the *81* interpretation followed here.

At this point the reliefs leave the emperor and his suite and *82* move to Dacia, showing a series of operations with roads and bridges in construction, trees being felled, and carpentry in progress, all carried out by men wearing a short, draped tunic, as the Roman *classiarii* probably did. One of them, an 'axe master' with his tool, is directing activities. It has been held that sailors specialized in this kind of work.

Now the hostilities of the second war begin. Dacian warriors, under the command of the *pilleati* chiefs, assemble at a large stone-walled fortress (Blidaru?) and then attack in force the Roman garrisons. *83*

(XV) The Romans are represented in shorthand by one *castellum* only, defended by auxiliaries, whose several shield-emblems (including those of a *milliaria*) indicate that they belong to many cohorts. While the auxiliary garrisons are engaged in the defence, the Dacians attack the powerful Roman camp at Drobetae. Decebalus' plan to cut the permanent bridge, by now nearly completed in place of the bridge of boats, becomes clear in the following scenes; and it was a logical aim, since this bridge was the hinge of the entire logistic system of the Roman expedition. *86–7*

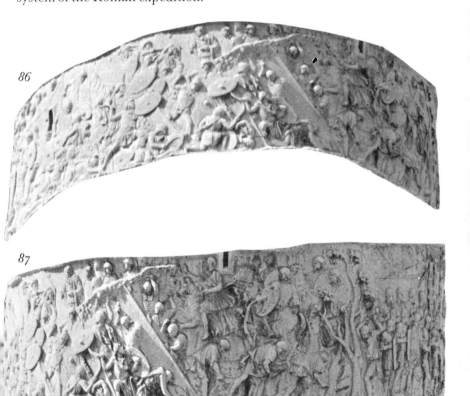

The attack of the Dacians is so violent that the legionaries
86   have to evacuate two walls. In spite of the intervention of the
       auxiliaries on one side and of a praetorian unit on the other, the
87–8   Romans are reduced to the last ditch, close to the bridge. This
       latter detail is brought out by the fact that the defenders of this
       final rampart are brandishing axes, which are the tools of the
       fabri (who were working at the superstructures of the bridge
       nearby) and are by no means the typical weapons of the
       legionaries. At this moment of mortal danger for the Romans,
87–8   the emperor reappears to save the situation, riding full gallop
       at the head of a body of auxiliary horsemen. Trajan, while
       coming as *deus ex machina* to Drobetae, rides down the Danube
       (and so backwards on the spiral) along a rocky ledge where
       three men are lined up respectively intent on felling a tree,
       cutting the rock, and squaring out a stone tablet, with the
       triumphant figure of the emperor above them.

           These pictorial details point to the road cut in the rock at the
       Danube's Iron Gates and widened by means of cantilevered
       planks supported on timber braces. The construction of this
       road, an outstanding achievement by the Roman military
       engineers, and its special features were described and com-
       memorated in the inscription on the stone *Tabula Traiana*,
       chiselled into the rocky side of the road (see p. 49).

           The emperor, at the head of a body of auxiliary cavalry
Figs. vii, no. 9, (three *alae*, at least) coming from Sirmium-Viminacium, hur-
viii, no. 22   riedly proceeds towards the endangered Drobetae along this

88

stretch of road, whose strategic importance has been pointed out.

The emperor's arrival as a *deus ex machina* has re-established the fortunes of the Roman army; and now legionaries and praetorians with their standards are gathered at the solemn ceremony of the consecration of Apollodorus' new bridge. This famous work is represented with great exactitude of detail; and we can readily distinguish the stone piers (only seven are represented, instead of the actual nineteen) from the super-structures with their wooden beams and railings. At either end we see the fortresses of Pontes and of Drobetae respectively.

The bridge forms the background for a ceremony of libation and augural sacrifices offered by Trajan himself, followed by a

88-9

89

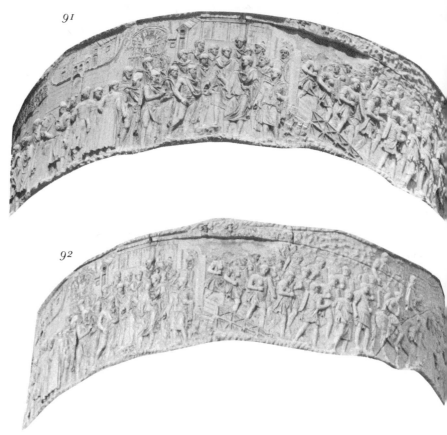

91

92

90 solemn reception of ambassadors. Before Drobetae and its amphitheatre (a construction usual in the Roman army's permanent camps), Trajan and the Roman staff (all wearing 90–1 the toga) are speaking with a group of barbarians whose costumes give us interesting ethnographical data.

They belong to the different populations who gravitated towards the Danubian basin: the Geto-Dacians, with their characteristic headgears; the Sarmato-Scythian Roxolani, with their long tunics; the Bastarnae (Germans), with their hair dressed in a lateral knot. The barbarians are dealing with the emperor on a level of equal dignity, and the scene seems to imply a significant contact of Rome with civilian and peaceful peoples from outside the Roman sphere, despite the impending war in this very area.

93

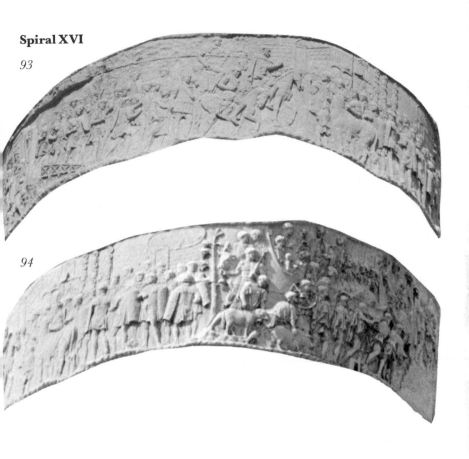

94

(XVI) In fact, immediately afterwards, the legionaries in marching-dress cross the Danube on the great bridge, through an arch adorned with the trophies of the first war and of the recent battle. Trajan rides at their head. It is the spring of AD 106. On the Dacian bank there soon occurs a meeting with another legionary contingent; and the *exercitus*, thus reunited, makes the usual ritual sacrifices before the camp (with *suovetaurilia* and music of military bands), within which is Trajan.

The *lustratio* ceremony is here, too, followed by the *adlocutio exercitus* with the emperor and his staff on a platform, exhorting the troops before the advance. The three standards held in front of the platform bear naval crowns, perhaps given to those troops who have distinguished themselves in 'amphibious' operations or in the construction and the defence of the bridge

91–2
93

94–5

95
95–6

at Drobetae. Next, Trajan is sitting inside the turreted walls of a camp, surrounded by his bodyguard of *equites singulares* (here on foot), as is demonstrated by the presence of oval shields with the relevant emblem and of the *vexillum*.

Fig. vii, no. 4

The advance begins, then, with the army divided into two groups, marching parallel to one another on the Column, while in reality they would have followed different routes: the one more direct, towards the north-east, the other longer and due east, with successive turnings to north and west.

97–8

It is likely, in fact, that after the experience of the first war, Trajan would have decided to block and invest Sarmizegetusa, again the stronghold of the Dacian resistance, from different sides. He therefore sends a body of troops along the Mehadia valley and the Teregova pass to reach the entrance to the Bistra valley, the route of the southern contingent during the first war.*

Fig. iii

This time the emperor places himself at the head of the army which takes the longer route along the valley of the Olt to attack Sarmizegetusa from the east and south. On the frieze, the first Roman body is shown below and is formed of auxiliaries and a minor contingent of praetorians, who are marching in line and are preceded by the standards and the military musicians. The second contingent, headed by Trajan, is marching on the upper part of the frieze and is mainly com-

100–1

97–8

*Recently, H. Daicoviciu and R. Florescu (*Römer in Rumänien*, Cologne, 1969, p. 35) have suggested that a western route was taken along the Mures (Marisus) valley.

96

97

98

posed of legionaries. It is counterbalanced by the scene of the
99 arrival in a camp, where the luggage, carried on mules and
wagons, is unpacked, while a few auxiliaries are drawing water
from a river. The bank, very steep, is surmounted by means of a
small ladder (to avoid making the water muddy?).

This 'upper' army, led by the emperor, is soon transferred to
another camp, whose gate is guarded by an auxiliary infantry-
101 man in full dress, as is evident from his crested helmet (the only
one on the frieze).

Spiral XVII

99

100

(XVII) Meanwhile, below the camp's wall, a long column of auxiliary troops is defiling ('lower' army), headed by oriental archers clad in long, swishing tunics and wearing conical caps *100–2* (or helmets); they probably belong to the *cohortes Ituraeorum* and *Hemesenorum (sagittariorum)* and are followed by bare-waisted *symmachiarii*.

After the representation of the two Roman contingents advancing separately there follows the unified scene of legionaries reaping the crops sown by the enemy, so as to *102* transport them to the camp (at the back), while the auxiliaries are watching. This indicates that the summer of year AD 106 has come.

The Roman menace is looming over Sarmizegetusa and the
103 Dacians assemble in the town or in a big citadel on a hilltop
(Blidaru?). Inside and outside the stone walls, chieftains and
warriors are angrily altercating with each other, an unfortu-
nate habit of the Thracians recorded by Tacitus (*Ann.* IV, 50).
C. and H. Daicoviciu (1966) suggested that the Dacian
garrison is debating the possibility of making a sally to help a
body of comrades in distress nearby. In fact, at the foot of the
104-5 hill the Roman vanguard, an auxiliary unit of light infantry

103

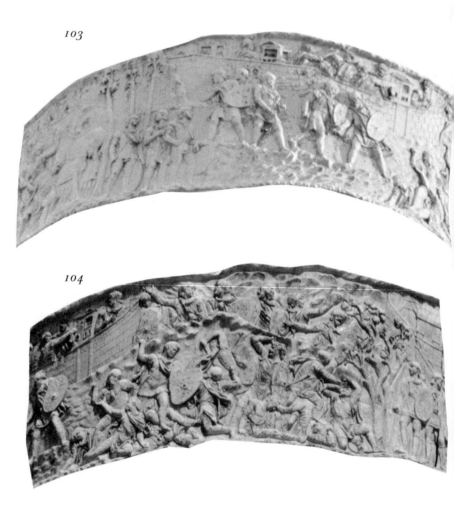

104

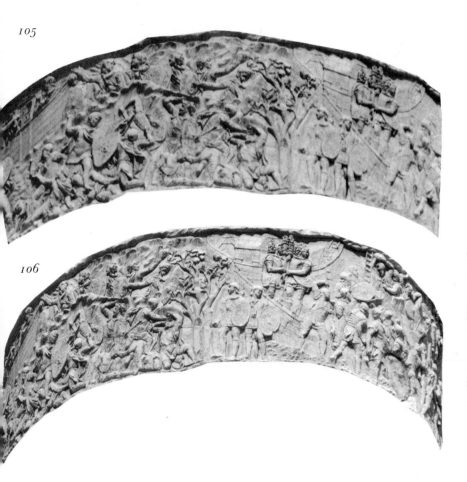

(without helmets), is overwhelming a Dacian rear-guard as it retreats towards Sarmizegetusa.

This is the first, and lower, Roman corps, that has taken the shorter way and is reaching the fortified outskirts of Sarmizegetusa on the western side. The auxiliary cohorts that, as we have already said, represent the principal force of this corps, are going to camp before the Dacian capital. While the *signiferi* are standing in front of the camp's gateways, the *auxilia* attack Sarmizegetusa's walls on the western side, where the rampart is a *murus Gallicus* (polygonal blocks held together by a framework of beams), defended by many Dacians. The Romans (auxiliary infantrymen and a few legionaries) mount

106

107–8

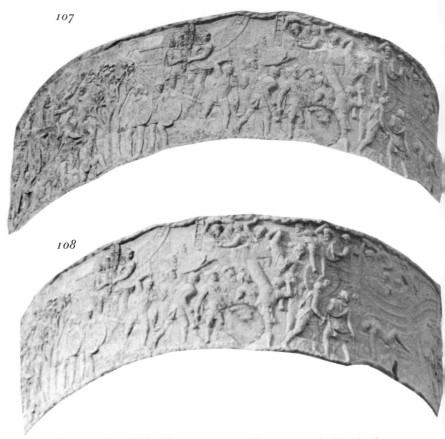

108–9   the attack with ladders, protected by a remarkable deployment of slingers (a *cohors funditorum*?), who have the task of keeping the Dacians away from the crenellated parapets of the massive wall.

109

22

109–10   (XVIII) The corpse of a Dacian warrior fallen before the walls is here exhibited with special emphasis: it reproduces, as regards both position and aspect, a figure in 'metope' XXVII of the Trophy at Adamklissi, and it could allude to some unrecorded personage or episode. Beyond this fallen man we can see the turreted walls of Sarmizegetusa rising above the folds of the mountains, with the auxiliary vanguard and a column of legionaries of the 'upper' army corps that has reached its objective from the east or south-east.

109

110

111

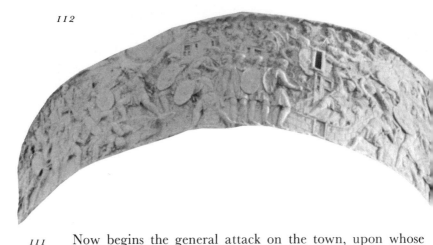

111
110–11
Now begins the general attack on the town, upon whose rocky glacis strange devices are seen, consisting of three rings placed at the corners of triangular trabeations, whose top is joined to rolls. Their significance has not yet been explained, but one should not rule out the possibility that they were designed for some form of signalling.

Figs. vii,
no. 6, viii,
nos. 16, 19,
x, nos. 32–3
111
111
The assault is led by many auxiliary cohorts, among which are one *voluntariorum c.R.*, one *torquata*, and by a strong body of *symmachiarii*, covered by archers, clad in scale-armour and wearing the conical helmet, similar to those seen at the attack on Piatra Rosie. The legionaries, too, resort to their *gladius*. The besieged defend themselves strenuously in one sector,

111–2
while farther on a party of them seems to have abandoned the battle and moved outside the walls: above there is great confusion.

Fig. vii, no. 6
112
112–3
114–5
Here a Dacian chief displays the captured shield of an auxiliary cohort *voluntariorum* (or *ingenuorum*) *c.R.*, adorned with the emblem of the thunderbolt (already seen among the Roman attackers). The Romans have obviously made a breach through the defences and the legionaries are intent on demolishing a stretch of the walls and on felling trees for the construction of new siege-machines. It is the beginning of the end: Dacian warriors are starting to surrender to Trajan, kneeling and asking for mercy in the presence of the auxiliaries.

116–7
(XIX) In the part of the town still in Dacian possession, the defenders, having by now lost any hope, set fire to the buildings.

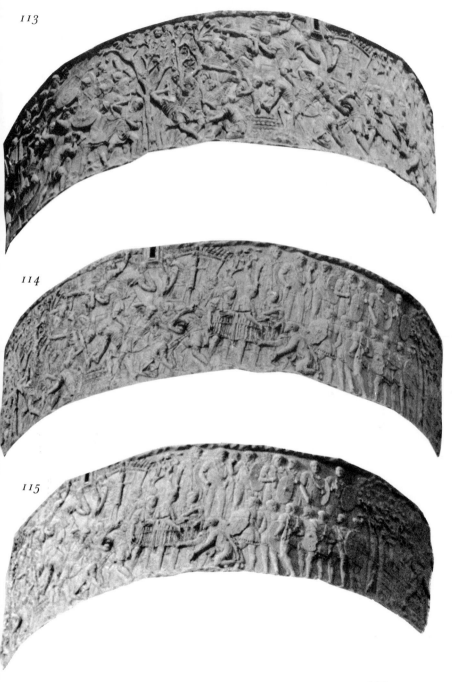

113

114

115

116

117

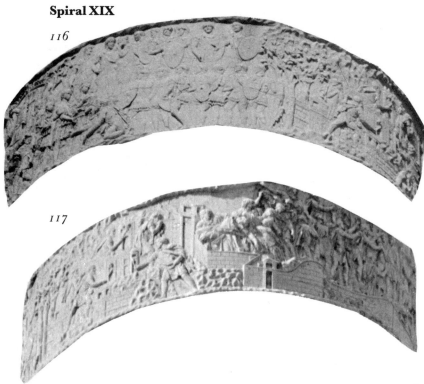

118–9 A group of Dacians prefers death to defeat, after the precepts of Zamolxis. Within the walls, with rounded corners corresponding to the terraces dug up recently on the site, a chief, standing up, drinks from a large pot of poison and hands it round to the warriors, noble cap-wearers as well as common *comati*, who seem to acclaim him before they die.

An alternative explanation of this scene has been put forward, suggesting that it could represent the desperate distribution of the last water left to the thirsty garrison, the Roman besiegers having cut off every source of it to the town. Tacitus (*Ann.* IV, 49), in describing the siege of a Thracian hill-fort by Sabinus' troops, lays emphasis on the lack of water in it after the Romans had severed the external supplies. It has been also demonstrated (C. Daicoviciu, 1954, p. 33) that the water supply to the Dacian *cetati* was generally inadequate.

The scene of a collective suicide, if it is such, probably taking place on the upper and 'sacred' terrace of Sarmizegetusa's en-

196

clave, is one of the most dramatic on the Column. The surviving
defenders try to save themselves by swift flight, while many   *119–20*
others continue to surrender to Trajan and the legionaries.   *121–2*
Decebalus, however, has evidently succeeded in escaping death
and capture.

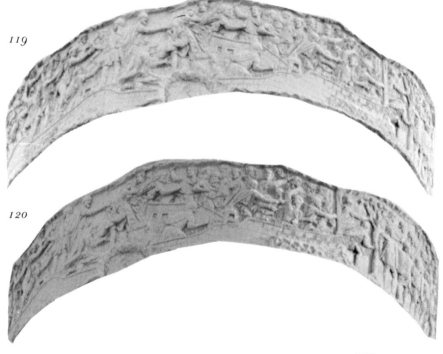

119

120

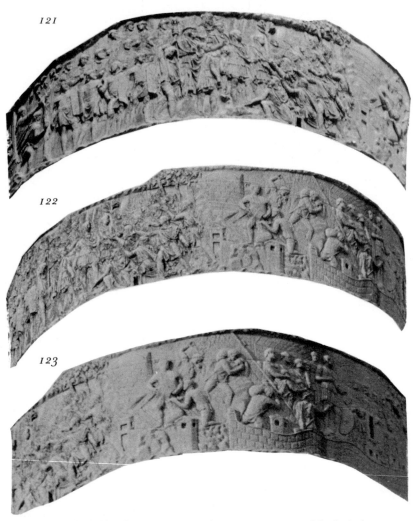

122–3
(XX) The Roman troops have now gone with their baggage
inside the walls of Sarmizegetusa, which has been divided into
two sectors, and they are given a *modius** of corn. Trajan,
standing on a platform together with officers and standard

*The *modius*, a measure of capacity (nine-tenths of a peck), was adopted by
the imperial authority as a symbol of 'abundant corn-supply' in coinage
celebrating *Frumenta, Annona*, etc. (See M. & S., Nerva: 52, 89, 109–13). Here
it hinted at the plentiful provisions captured in Sarmizegetusa and distributed
to the Roman soldiers.

bearers, here receives the fifth (?) imperial *salutatio* from his legionaries, praetorians and auxiliaries. It is either September 124 or October AD 106.

The advance now goes on towards the north-western 125 Carpathians. Legionaries cut out a road in the woods and build 126

Spiral XX

124

125

126

127
camps and defences, while the auxiliaries fulfil covering duties

Fig. viii,
no. 13
(there is a *cohors torquata*). Once again, three Dacian chieftains
kneel down in front of Trajan. This scene may, perhaps, represent the giving of information by Bicilis, who revealed to the

128
Romans the place wherein a great treasure was hidden by
Decebalus before he fled (an episode quoted by Dio, LXVIII,
14, 4–5).

Fig. viii,
no. 13
A strong body of auxiliary cohorts, with soldiers displaying
variously adorned shields (one with a *torques*-crown), crosses a

129
wide river on a rough bridge composed of four planks nailed to
vertical poles (hinting at unskilled auxiliary bridge-making?)

and proceeds towards the north-west. It is likely that the scene represents the crossing of the river Marisus (Mures), which was the major water-barrier on the way to the central districts of Carpathian Dacia and to the towns of Apulum, Napoca and Potaissa. At this point, however, the Dacians resume the offensive and make an attack in force on a Roman camp *130* (probably a 'shorthand' rendering of several camps); this is *131–2* located at the confluence of two rivers (the Marisus and a southern tributary), and garrisoned by three auxiliary co-horts, one of which is a *milliaria*, that fiercely resist, even throw- *132–3* ing squared stone-blocks at the assailants.

130

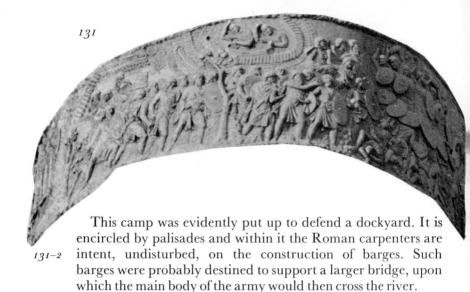

131-2 This camp was evidently put up to defend a dockyard. It is encircled by palisades and within it the Roman carpenters are intent, undisturbed, on the construction of barges. Such barges were probably destined to support a larger bridge, upon which the main body of the army would then cross the river.

Spiral XXI

132

133

(XXI) This last and unsuccessful Dacian assault is led by
Decebalus himself, who watches it from a woody hill-top beyond   *133*
which his surviving warriors will eventually retire. The defen-   *133-4*
sive victory of the Romans is celebrated with an imperial
adlocutio delivered to auxiliaries and legionaries. The scene   *135*

135

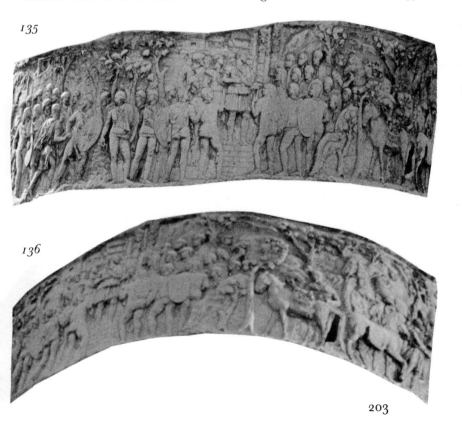

136

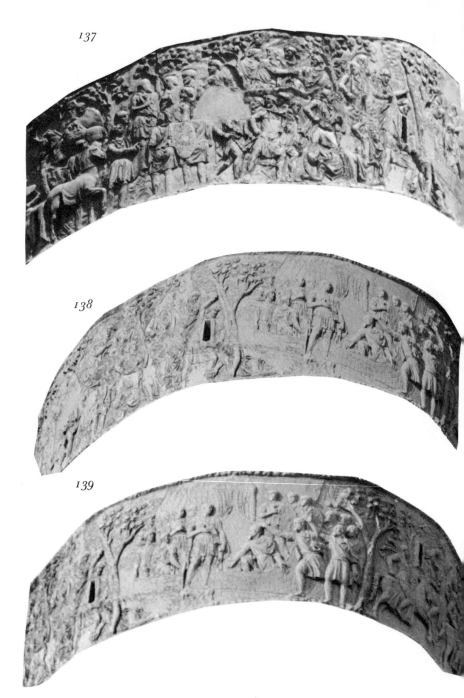

137

138

139

140

141

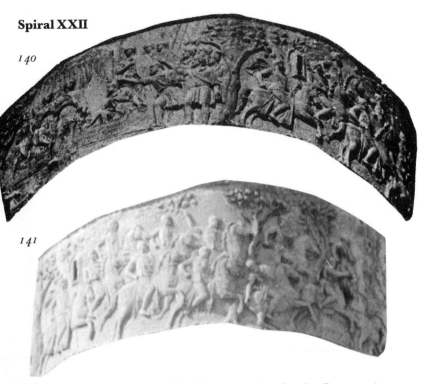

follows on the capture and loading on mules, by the Romans in
the presence of unarmed Dacians, of Decebalus' treasure (cups,   *135–6*
plates, etc.). According to Dio's history, this was buried in the
Sargetia's (Apa Gradistei's?) bed, the stream having been
temporarily diverted. But the hiding place had been revealed
to the Romans by Bicilis (see above). It is well known, moreover, that the Romans seized in Dacia an enormous booty in
the form of precious metals.

The indomitable Decebalus understands now that everything is lost: he gathers around him his devoted followers and
addresses them for the last time. What he said is easy to imagine,   *137*
since many Dacians again prefer death to surrender and kill
one another with swords and spears, while some of them go to   *137–8*
the Roman camp and submit to Trajan, offering him gifts in
front of the imperial *praetorium*.   *138–9*

(XXII) Decebalus and a few Dacian survivors flee once more   *140–3*
on horseback, closely pursued by auxiliary *alae* (among which

142

143

Figs. ix,
no. 29, vii,
no. 13
143–4 is one *bistorquata*) and by a cohort (probably *equitata*) that reach and surround the Dacian king in a thick forest: faithful to his creed he commits suicide by cutting his throat rather than fall into the hands of the enemy. One might well quote Winston Churchill: 'unconquerable except by death, which does not count in honour'.

Two boys (Decebalus' sons?) and a young man are, however, captured.

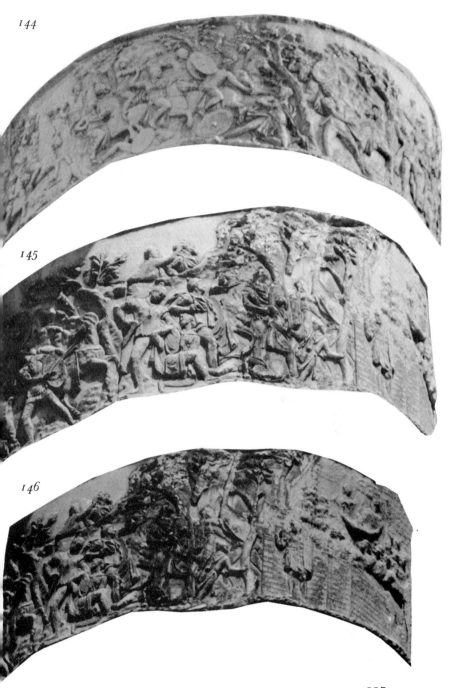

147

148

146-8 The imperial camp is now the scene of a grim spectacle, watched by the praetorians, as two soldiers present to the assembled troops the severed head of Decebalus, laid on a tray. The head will be sent to Rome. It is probable that on this occasion Trajan was acclaimed *imperator* for the sixth time.

149-50 (XXIII) The auxiliaries continue to advance and mop up the occupied territories, capturing prisoners and meeting with little resistance. The Romans are by now in the northern districts of Dacia. A little lake is shown amid the woods, rich in
150 game (deer and boars), a common scene in the Carpathian mountains.

149

150

151

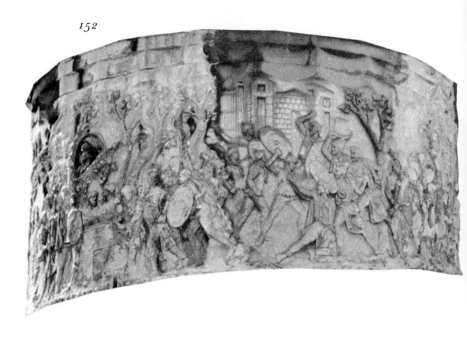

150–1
A forest god looks from a niche at Dacian prisoners, brought from all sides to the Roman camp. A last centre of resistance is under the walls of a town (Napoca, Potaissa?) on the most distant frontier of Dacia where the buildings already have a foreign look. Here warriors armed with scythes and led by a young chief are fighting fiercely against Roman auxiliaries among which are a unit *torquata* and one *c.R. ingenuorum*. The attitude of this chief, who is killed on the spot by the spear (lost)

152–3
of an auxiliary, is quite similar to that of the dying Decebalus and perhaps indicates that he is another son of the Dacian king. Here also, some warriors who are fighting at the side of the Dacians wear conical helmets and should be regarded as Roxolan borderers. After the victory the same auxiliaries set the

153–4
154–5
town on fire. The war is over: Dacia has fallen and its inhabitants are driven away, while a group of bearded men, wearing a short tunic, a cloak *(paenula)* and military boots *(caligae)* come in. They are clearly indicated as ageing soldiers in 'undress' uniform, very probably the veterans to whom land has been assigned in the new province of Dacia so as to colonize and Romanize the country.

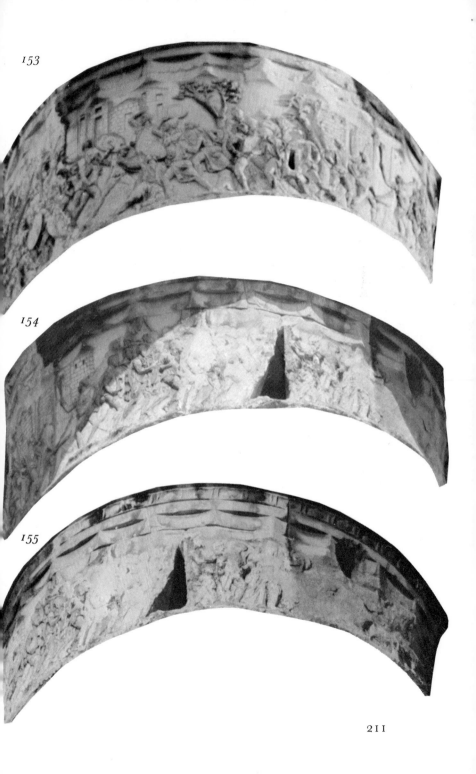

156   The last scene* is the touching one of the native folk, men burdened with packages, women and children, abandoning their country in front of and beyond the mountains. They drive their cattle ahead and look back at the lost motherland, facing with dauntless pride the incoming Roman settlers.

Here we have the final tribute that the Column pays to the indomitable Dacians. This very scene, from the Column's marble scroll, merges into the life and history of Rumania up to the present day.

157   Then the spiral grows narrower, while sheep placidly graze around young trees, sprouting anew from the barren soil of *Dacia Augusta Provincia*, below Trajan's image set up on the Column's summit in the heart of Rome for the centuries to come.

*Since this important scene on the Column is now badly damaged, its details can be better observed on a copy engraved about a century ago.

APPENDIXES
BIBLIOGRAPHY
INDEX

APPENDIX A

Dio Cassius' commentary on the Dacian wars.
The following extracts from *Dio's Roman History*, bk. LXVIII,
are reproduced by kind permission of the Loeb Classical
Library, vol. 8.

(6) After spending some time in Rome Trajan made a campaign against the Dacians; for he took into account their past
deeds and was grieved at the amount of money they were receiving annually, and he also observed that their power and
their pride were increasing. Decebalus, learning of his advance,
became frightened, since he well knew that on the former
occasion it was not the Romans that he had conquered, but
Domitian, whereas now he would be fighting against both
Romans and Trajan, the emperor. . . .

(8) For these reasons, then, Decebalus had good cause to fear
him. When Trajan in his campaign against the Dacians had
drawn near Tapae, where the barbarians were encamped, a
large mushroom was brought to him on which was written in
Latin characters a message to the effect that the Buri and other
allies advised Trajan to turn back and keep the peace. Nevertheless he engaged the foe, and saw many wounded on his own
side and killed many of the enemy. And when the bandages gave
out, he is said not to have spared even his own clothing, but to
have cut it up into strips. In honour of the soldiers who had died
in the battle he ordered an altar to be erected and funeral rites
to be performed annually.

(9) Decebalus had sent envoys even before his defeat, not the
long-haired men this time, as before, but the noblest among the
cap-wearers. These threw down their arms, and casting themselves upon the ground, begged Trajan that, if possible, Decebalus himself should be permitted to meet and confer with him,
promising that he would do everything that was commanded;

or, if not, that someone at least should be sent to agree upon terms with him. Those sent were Sura and Claudius Livianus, the prefect; but nothing was accomplished, since Decebalus did not dare to meet them either, but sent envoys also on this occasion. Trajan seized some fortified mountains and on them found the arms and the captured engines, as well as the standard which had been taken in the time of Fuscus. Decebalus, because of this, coupled with the fact that Maximus had at this same time captured his sister and also a strong position, was ready to agree without exception to every demand that had been made – not that he intended to abide by his agreement, but in order that he might secure a respite from his temporary reverses. So he reluctantly engaged to surrender his arms, engines and engine-makers, to give back the deserters, to demolish the forts, to withdraw from captured territory, and furthermore to consider the same persons enemies and friends as the Romans did, and neither to give shelter to any of the deserters nor to employ any soldier from the Roman empire; for he had been acquiring the largest and best part of his force by persuading men to come to him from Roman territory. This was after he had come to Trajan, fallen upon the ground and done obeisance and thrown away his arms. He also sent envoys in the matter to the senate, in order that he might secure the ratification of the peace by that body. After concluding this compact the emperor left the camp at Sarmizegetusa, and having stationed garrisons here and there throughout the remainder of the territory, returned to Italy.

(10) The envoys from Decebalus, upon being brought into the senate, laid down their arms, clasped their hands in the attitude of captives, and spoke some words of supplication; thus they obtained peace and received back their arms. Trajan celebrated a triumph and was given the title of Dacicus. . . .

Inasmuch as Decebalus was reported to him to be acting contrary to the treaty in many ways, was collecting arms, receiving those who deserted, repairing the forts, sending envoys to his neighbours and injuring those who had previously differed with him, even going so far as to annex a portion of the territory of the Iazyges (which Trajan later would not give back to them when they asked for it), therefore the senate again declared him an enemy, and Trajan once more conducted the war against him in person instead of entrusting it to others.

(11) As numerous Dacians kept transferring their allegiance to Trajan, and also for certain other reasons, Decebalus again sued for peace. But since he could not be persuaded to surrender both his arms and himself, he proceeded openly to collect troops and summon the surrounding nations to his aid, declaring that if they deserted him they themselves would be imperilled, and that it was safer and easier for them, by fighting on his side before suffering any harm, to preserve their freedom, than if they should allow his people to be destroyed and then later be subjugated themselves when bereft of allies.

Though Decebalus was faring badly in open conflict, nevertheless by craft and deceit he almost compassed Trajan's death. He sent into Moesia some deserters to see if they could make away with him, inasmuch as the emperor was generally accessible and now, on account of the exigencies of warfare, admitted to a conference absolutely every one who desired it. But they were not able to carry out this plan, since one of them was arrested on suspicion and under torture revealed the entire plot.

(12) Decebalus then sent an invitation to Longinus, a leader of the Roman army who had made himself a terror to the king in the wars, and persuaded him to meet him, on the pretext that he would do whatever should be demanded. He then arrested him and questioned him publicly about Trajan's plans, and when Longinus refused to admit anything, he took him about with him under guard, though not in bonds. And sending an envoy to Trajan, he asked that he might receive back his territory as far as the Ister and be indemnified for all the money he had spent on the war, in return for restoring Longinus to him. An ambiguous answer was returned, of such a nature as not to cause Decebalus to believe that Trajan regarded Longinus as either of great importance or yet of slight importance, the object being to prevent his being destroyed, on the one hand, or being preserved to them on excessive terms, on the other. So Decebalus delayed, still considering what he should do. In the meantime Longinus, having secured poison with the aid of the freedman, promised Decebalus to win Trajan over, hoping the king would thus have no suspicion of what he was going to do and so would not keep a very strict watch over him; also, in order to enable the freedman to gain safety, he wrote a letter containing a petition in his behalf and gave it to him to carry to Trajan. Then, when the other had gone, he drank the poison at night

and died. Thereupon Decebalus demanded the freedman from Trajan, promising to give him in return the body of Longinus and ten captives. He at once sent the centurion who had been captured with Longinus, in order that he might arrange the matter; and it was from the centurion that the whole story of Longinus was learned. However, Trajan neither sent him back nor surrendered the freedman, deeming his safety more important for the dignity of the empire than the burial of Longinus.

(13) Trajan constructed over the Ister a stone bridge for which I cannot sufficiently admire him. Brilliant, indeed, as are his other achievements, yet this surpasses them. For it has twenty piers of squared stone one hundred and fifty feet in height above the foundations and sixty in width, and these, standing at a distance of one hundred and seventy feet from one another, are connected by arches. How, then, could one fail to be astonished at the expenditure made upon them, or at the way in which each of them was placed in a river so deep, in water so full of eddies, and on a bottom so muddy? For it was impossible, of course, to divert the stream anywhere. I have spoken of the width of the river; but the stream is not uniformly so narrow, since it covers in some places twice, and in others thrice as much ground, but the narrowest point and the one in that region best suited to building a bridge has the width named. Yet the very fact that the river in its descent is here contracted from a great flood to such a narrow channel, after which it again expands into a greater flood, makes it all the more violent and deep, and this feature must be considered in estimating the difficulty of constructing the bridge. This too, then, is one of the achievements that show the magnitude of Trajan's designs, though the bridge is of no use to us; for merely the piers are standing, affording no means of crossing, as if they had been erected for the sole purpose of demonstrating that there is nothing which human ingenuity cannot accomplish. Trajan built the bridge because he feared that some time when the Ister was frozen over war might be made upon the Romans on the further side, and he wished to facilitate access to them by this means. Hadrian, on the contrary, was afraid that it might also make it easy for the barbarians, once they had overpowered the guard at the bridge, to cross into Moesia, and so he removed the superstructure.

(14) Trajan, having crossed the Ister by means of this bridge, conducted the war with safe prudence rather than with haste, and eventually, after a hard struggle, vanquished the Dacians. In the course of the campaign he himself performed many deeds of good generalship and bravery, and his troops ran many risks and displayed great prowess on his behalf. It was here that a certain horseman, after being carried, badly wounded, from the battle in the hope that he could be healed, when he found that he could not recover, rushed from his tent (for his injury had not yet reached his heart) and, taking his place once more in the line, perished after displaying great feats of valour. Decebalus, when his capital and all his territory had been occupied and he was himself in danger of being captured, committed suicide; and his head was brought to Rome. In this way Dacia became subject to the Romans, and Trajan founded cities there. The treasures of Decebalus were also discovered, though hidden beneath the river Sargetia, which ran past his palace. With the help of some captives Decebalus had diverted the course of the river, made an excavation in its bed, and into the cavity had thrown a large amount of silver and gold and other objects of great value that could stand a certain amount of moisture; then he had heaped stones over them and piled on earth, afterwards bringing the river back into its course. He also had caused the same captives to deposit his robes and other articles of a like nature in caves, and after accomplishing this had made away with them to prevent them from disclosing anything. But Bicilis, a companion of his who knew what had been done, was seized and gave information about these things.

APPENDIX B

Dacian hill-forts

It has been mentioned (p. 33) that the Dacians laid down a system of hill-forts covering the approaches to the highland core of their country and to their capital Sarmizegetusa. Such forts were built at key-points guarding the access, from north, west and south, to the upper valley of the Apa Gradistei.

On the south the belt of hill-forts was also reinforced by a stronghold on the plain at Trojan de Cioclovina (a few miles south of Piatra Rosie), intended to bar the route from the upper Jiu valley. Furthermore, the most western approach to Sarmizegetusa, by way of the Bistra valley, was sealed by the defences laid across the Transylvanian Iron Gates at Tapae. Sarmizegetusa itself was heavily fortified.

The Thracians generally defended their rough home-country by fortifying steep hill-tops, either putting up strong palisades or building permanent 'castles' in stonework, or making use of both devices. These practices are mentioned by ancient authors (Jordanes, Florus, quoted by Davies, p. 78) and more precisely by Tacitus when dealing with the Thracian revolt against the Romans in AD 26 (*Ann.* IV, 46–49). The careful studies and excavations carried out by C. Daicoviciu (1943, 1954, 1955, 1963) on the sites of such hill-forts and at Sarmizegetusa, when compared with the relevant reliefs on the column, seem to make possible a fresh approach to some very important problems of the Dacian wars. It is therefore proposed to devote some space to these Dacian 'citadels' *(cetati)*.

Attention will be focused upon the forts at Piatra Rosie, Costesti, Blidaru and on the walls of Sarmizegetusa, in order to examine the technique of their construction, their plan and layout, and their identification on the Column. The Dacian walled posts and towns in the Banat are not considered here, since they lack the characteristics of hill-forts proper, and actually exhibit a Daco-Roman element in their structures (see Davies, p. 83, for Arcidava and Tibiscum).

As regards the technique of construction, the usual siting of the hill-forts was at the top of steep cliffs, with a belt of walls or stockades that enclosed part of the slopes. The ramparts were reinforced with towers, either of wood or stone, and had thatched gabled roofs and open fronts or small windows. Isolated towers outside the forts often provided external defence. Inside the walls there were other towers, houses and huts for the garrison, and accommodation for the cattle and supplies. The ramparts of the 'permanent' citadels were of two main types. One was composed of blocks of limestone, measuring about $2 \times 2 \times 1$ feet, accurately fitted to one another in close-set rows; the other was the so-called *murus Gallicus* (described by Caesar in *Bell. Gall.* VII, 23), which consisted of polygonal or square slabs of masonry divided horizontally by a strong framework of beams passing through the wall from back to front and held in place by longitudinal beams; the space between the inner and outer edifices was filled with smaller, irregular stones. Richmond (1935, pp. 38, 39) stressed the remarkable precision with which ramparts of this latter type are represented on the Column in the scenes of the siege of Sarmizegetusa. Examples are to be found in some native strongholds of the Iron Age in Britain and on the Continent. But walls of masonry are in the minority.

Semi-permanent defences were produced by putting up a strong palisade, sometimes combined with, or resting on, stretches of the *murus Gallicus*. Such wooden stockades were often added to 'permanent' castles, perhaps when the defences of vital posts had to be enlarged or strengthened in a hurry in the face of impending danger. A situation of this kind is vividly illustrated by the fort at Piatra Rosie, both on the Column and on the actual site (see p. 168). Since stone and wooden walls had to be adapted to rough ground and to slopes, level terraces were created and staircases frequently built to connect different parts of the ramparts and towers. The gateways were few and small, and on the Column these are often represented with a gabled roof. Ditches were unnecessary around walls that stood directly above steep slopes or sheer precipices. On the other hand, in the case of barrages in gorges (e.g. Tapae) or of fortifications of flat sites, dry ditches were dug and crossed by narrow bridges leading to the gateways. Complicated external defences were also added, for instance, strong poles protruding from the ground *(cippi)* to counteract cavalry charges and traps in the form of hidden pits containing sharpened stakes *(lilia)*. All these devices are clearly visible on the Column's frieze.

The outlines of the Dacian citadels varied considerably, as will be seen later. On the whole, it seems that their design generally followed the shapes of the hill-tops and the needs of the moment rather than some preconceived common pattern. At any rate, the dominating positions and the defensive works characteristic of these forts contributed to the creation of formidable strongholds, which could only have been captured by a very high expenditure of lives and effort on the part of the Roman attackers. This is clearly shown in the relevant scenes on the Column.

A major problem for all these Dacian citadels was that of water supply. Springs and wells were lacking on the hill-tops and water had to be carried in by pipes from nearby mountains (e.g. at Piatra Rosie) or rain water had to be collected and stored in cisterns and jars (e.g. at Blidaru). This grave handicap was probably complicated by the fact that cattle were often driven into the forts for the purposes of protection and food supply. This obviously increased the demand for water. The menace of thirst was always impending in time of siege as a result of the cutting off of the external water supply or of drought.

Another common feature of the hill-forts was the presence of religious buildings ('sanctuaries') inside or near the citadel.

Only four forts are well known to date, and they will now be considered in turn as a preliminary to their critical comparison with individual scenes on the Column.

COSTESTI, built on the hill of Cetatuia (1,700 feet) to bar the entrance to the Apa Gradistei valley, comprised two main towers of limestone blocks, the first floors of which were reached from inside and outside by stone staircases and served as living quarters. In the basement supplies were stored. Between these towers there was a watch turret. The defensive system consisted of a double stockade of stout poles surrounding the flattened hill-top and the inhabited towers. A stretch of huge stone wall, nine feet thick, was added on the south-eastern side alone, since elsewhere the sheer cliff was sufficient defence. This wall was supplied with three massive bastions. On the western side there was a single bastion; on the northern side were two watch turrets; and, facing east, a larger tower. It is, moreover, likely that earth was heaped up all round the hill-top. Three sanctuaries outside, and one sanctuary inside the fortifications, have been excavated.

BLIDARU, a typical permanent castle, has left imposing ruins about one mile south of Costesti, on a hill 2,100 feet high and also dominating the upper Apa Gradistei. It consisted of two defensive systems, complementary to one another, with several watch-towers outside the walls. The castle proper was quadrangular with stone walls, towers at the corners and a larger, square, inhabited tower inside. The annexed defences were roughly triangular in shape and consisted of a double limestone wall, with strong-rooms on two storeys, a fighting platform, and store-rooms underneath. As at Piatra Rosie, a unique complex resulted, completely subdivided by the western wall of the main castle. A great cistern was dug out on the western side of the hill.

PIATRA ROSIE (the 'Red Rock') was built on a steep hill-top surrounded by reddish cliffs at an altitude of about 2,500 feet above the valley of the Luncani. It consisted of a permanent stone castle, rectangular in shape at the top, with five towers, to which was annexed a broader quadrangular palisade-fort with rounded corners and two towers. One watch-tower was also placed outside the walls. Within the permanent castle there was a wooden building erected on stone foundations and surrounded by a balcony. Outside, a small 'sanctuary' has been identified (see C. Daicoviciu, 1954). Altogether the two parts composed a fortress of a unique type divided into two by the eastern stone wall, with its gateway, of the permanent castle.

SARMIZEGETUSA. The scanty ruins of the Dacian capital have been found at the bottom of the Apa Gradistei valley (Gradistea Muncelului), on the hill of Gradistei (3,600 feet high). The town was protected by a long wall that followed the rising terrain and had a roughly rectangular shape, with the longer sides bent inwards and the two main gateways facing west and east. No remnants of towers have been found so far, but on the Column Sarmizegetusa's ramparts appear with spaced stone and wooden turrets and with various stretches in stonework and *murus Gallicus*. There are more extensive remains of two important 'sanctuaries' built on terraces outside the city wall on the east. These consist of circular and rectangular platforms along which pillars are aligned at regular intervals, probably according to the arrangement of a sun-calendar. These discoveries throw new light on problems in Dacian religion and astronomy (see C. Daicoviciu, 1955, 1963).

To sum up, there are two main types of Dacian hill-fort that required different representations on the Column's frieze. The sculptural rendering of fortifications in the background of the scenes is usually achieved by showing defence-walls, of one or two of these types, combined with a visual suggestion of the actual plan of the entire fort. Actually, the palisades, the stone-wall and the *murus Gallicus* are very clearly depicted, in some cases together with a *vol d'oiseau* glimpse of the citadel's outline, or of the slopes followed by the wall.

Since only two of the hill-forts examined were wholly of the stone-work (permanent) type, it could be argued that the Dacian strongholds represented on the Column in scenes relating to central Dacia, which were defended all round by walls of stone blocks, refer to Blidaru and to Sarmizegetusa. The identification of Sarmizegetusa is indeed obvious, at least in the classic scenes of its siege and capture during the second war, while that of Blidaru has never been attempted on the lines of these criteria.

It is probable that Blidaru is first clearly hinted at in the scene that represents Dacians in the act of demolishing the walls, made of stone blocks, of a citadel, in order to fulfil the armistice conditions dictated by the Romans at the end of the first war. This accords with the fact that defence structures of wood were more simply destroyed by fire, as the findings at Piatra Rosie (C. Daicoviciu, 1954) demonstrated. Another scene in which Blidaru could be identified is that of Dacian warriors rushing into a fortress to gather round their chieftain (possibly Decebalus), at the onset of the second war. The stronghold is completely walled with stone blocks, has an odd shape, and is subdivided in a way that recalls the actual plan of Blidaru.

On the other hand, when palisaded ramparts appear on the Column as protection for Dacian strongholds, either alone or combined with stone-walls, the other type of hill-forts ('temporary' or 'semi-permanent') seems to be hinted at, namely the type of Piatra Rosie and Costesti. The identification of the 'double fort' of Piatra Rosie can be arrived at with a reasonable degree of certainty in a scene on the Column in which the presence of a stone staircase is also emphasized (see p. 168–9). As far as Costesti is concerned, any indication of it on the Column remains a matter of speculation. But in view of the fact that this citadel guarded the actual entrance of the Apa Gradistei valley, it could well have been represented earlier than the other forts in the series of scenes showing attacks carried out by the Romans on the chain of hill-forts defending the valley.

Attempts at identifying Dacian strongholds by the above criteria must, however, take into consideration the possibility that other hill-forts (mostly of perishable wood) so far little known (e.g. Anines-Vîrfu lui Hulpe) or unknown, may well have had their place on the frieze.

APPENDIX C

Detailed discussion of the shield-emblems will be found in Chapter V. In this Appendix are summarized the main devices cited by letters and numbers in Chapter VIII.

Legionaries and Praetorians

The emblems indicated by italic capitals belong to legionary and/or praetorian units and are therefore displayed on quadrangular shields. From A to L (with the exception of G) they consist of variations on the basic motif of the thunderbolt-and-lightning, either with lateral wings or without them (H, I). This device is symbolic of the concept of Roman imperial divine might; it was probably intended to emphasize the specially close link which bound the legionaries and praetorians to Rome and the emperor. The emblems M and N consist of leaf-crowns, indicating glory and victory and possibly hinting at the most 'Trajanic' and 'victorious' of all the legions that fought in the Dacian wars, namely the XXX $Ulpia$ $Victrix$. G is the only shield that is devoid of symbolic significance; and this may perhaps represent an 'erasing' of the original emblem of a dishonoured legion $(XXI$ $Rapax?)$, which suffered $damnatio$ $memoriae$.

Auxilia and Symmachiarii

The emblems indicated by Arabic numbers belong to regular auxiliaries (1 to 30) and to irregular $symmachiarii$ (31 to 35), and are therefore represented on oval shields. 8 and 30 alone appear on the quadrangular shields of two $cohortes$ $scutatae$. The motifs 1, 2 and 3, with the Roman eagle, seem to belong to units which were granted the Roman citizenship for outstanding gallantry. From 4 to 8 the symbols are basically identical with those of the legionaries and praetorians (thunderbolt-and-lightning, except in the case of *5*). This probably indicates that the relevant units shared both true Roman origin and imperial status with the legionaries and praetorians, as did the Italian cohorts and the *alae civium Romanorum (voluntariorum)*, *ingenuorum, campestres,* and the *singulares* of the imperial bodyguard. The shields *9* to *18* and *26* to *30* show various crowns and wreaths in single or double circles and combined with stars, crescents and ribbons. All these seem to symbolize such military decorations as *coronae, torques* (the leaves-and-flowers wreath) and *armillae,* as well as the titles *torquata* (or *bistorquata*) and *armillata,* awarded to entire units for valour. The emblems *19* (the *pelta* of Thracian origin) to *25* (stars, crescents, flowers, horns below concentric discs, possibly Celtic) are of uncertain significance. The motifs *31* to *35,* displayed on the shields of the bare-chested *symmachiarii,* are very plain in character: a star, a crescent and two rings linked together (indicating the chains of slaves or prisoners or barbarian ornament?). *35* is rather more elaborate, but appears to be meaningless.

For the possible attribution of some of these shield-emblems to individual units, see p. 114–17.

APPENDIX D

Maximus, captor of Decebalus

The portrayal on the Column of the dying Decebalus (p. 207, *144*) now receives a companion picture, provided by the dramatic discovery of the tombstone of the Roman soldier who actually captured the king. It was found in Macedonia near Philippi in 1965 and has been published by M. Speidel (*Journal of Roman Studies*, lx [1970], pp. 142–53), to whose account this present note is deeply indebted.

The large grey marble stone (some 9 by 3 feet) bears a Latin inscription below two reliefs. The upper and larger relief shows a galloping auxiliary cavalryman, helmeted and cloaked, with two spears in his left hand and a drawn sword in his right hand; at his feet lies a bearded and trousered figure in a Dacian cap who sinks back dying, mouth open, and his curved sword with which he has just cut his throat is falling from his hand. The smaller relief represents two *torques* (necklaces) and two *armillae* (arm-rings).

The long inscription records the name and career of the hero: Tiberius Claudius Maximus, distinguished as legionary and auxiliary cavalryman, up to the rank of *decurio*. Maximus took part in the Dacian campaigns of both Domitian and Trajan, twice earning from the emperors the *dona militaria* which are depicted on his tombstone. Selected from Ala II Pannoniorum to serve as an *explorator* (*exploratores* were a special corps of mounted scouts), apparently as a *duplicarius exploratorum* or second-in-command of a troop, he led the men who actually captured Decebalus; he then brought the king's head to Trajan's camp at Ranisstorum (a site otherwise unknown).

Between the scene on the tombstone and that on the Column there is a slight difference. On the former Maximus is waving his sword, whereas on the latter he is stretching out his arm,

229

apparently trying to stop Decebalus from committing suicide and to capture him alive.

We know that the king's head was later sent to Rome (Dio Cassius, lviii.14.3; Fasti Ostienses ad AD 106), and the Column (*146–8*) shows that before this it was displayed to the assembled troops by two men. M. Speidel suggests that one was Trajan himself, at the final *adlocutio* which marked the end of the war.

ABBREVIATIONS

Arrian	Flavius, Arrianus, *Tactica*
BMC	British Museum catalogue
Caesar, *Bell. Gall.*	Gaius Julius Caesar, *De Bello Gallico*
CIL	*Corpus Inscriptionum Latinarum*
Cohen	H. Cohen, *Description historique des monnais frappées sous l'Empire Romain* (Paris 1880)
Digest	Justinian I, *Digesta*
Dio	Dio Cassius, *Roman History*
ILS	*Inscriptiones Latinae Selectae*, ed. H. Dessau (1892-1916)
Josephus	Flavius Josephus, *The Jewish War*
M. & S.	H. Mattingly and E. A. Sydenham, *Roman Imperial Coinage* (2nd ed. London 1962)
Pauly-Wissowa	*Realencyclopädie der klassischen Altertumswissenschaft*
Tacitus, *Ann.*	Cornelius Tacitus, *Annals*
Tacitus, *Germ.*	Cornelius Tacitus, *Germania*
Tacitus, *Hist.*	Cornelius Tacitus, *Histories*
Vegetius	Flavius Vegetius, *De Re Militari*
Virgil, *Georg.*	Virgil, *Georgics*

References to books listed in the Bibliography are identified in the text by the author's name and, where necessary, the date of publication.

BIBLIOGRAPHY

Baatz, D.,· 'Zur Geschutzbewaffnung römischer Auxiliartruppen in der frühen und mittleren Kaiserzeit', *Bonner Jahrbuch 166* (1966) 194

Baradez, J., 'Tropaeum Traiani', *Provincialia* (Basle-Stuttgart 1968)

Brilliant, R., 'Gesture and Rank in Roman Art', *Memoirs of the Connecticut Academy Arts & Sciences* vol. 14 (1963)

Cheesman, G., *The Auxilia of the Roman Imperial Army* (Oxford 1914)

Cichorius, C., *Die Reliefs des Trajanssäule* (Berlin 1886-1900)

Daicoviciu, C., *La Transilvania Romana* (Bucharest 1943)

Cetatea Dacica da Piatra Rosie (Bucharest 1954)

231

'Santierul archeologic Gradistea Muncelului-Blidarul', *Studii si cercetari de istorie vece 6* (1955) 195

Dacia Libera si Dacia Romana (Bucharest 1964)

'Trésors archeologiques de la Transylvanie', *Archeologia* 28 (1969) 58–67

Daicoviciu, C., and Daicoviciu, H., *Sarmizegetusa* (Russian text, Bucharest 1963)

Columna lui Traian (Bucharest 1966)

Daicoviciu, H., *Dacii* (Bucharest 1968)

Daris, S., *Documenti per la storia dell'esercito Romano in Egitto* (Milan 1964)

Davies, G. A. T., 'Trajan's First Dacian War', *Journal of Roman Studies* VII (1917) 74-97

Dobson, B., in V. Domaszewski *Die Rangordnung des römischen Heeres* (3rd ed. Cologne 1967)

Domaszewski, A. von, *Die Rangordnung der römischen Heeres* (2nd ed. Cologne 1964)

Durry, M., *Les cohortes prétoriennes* (Paris 1938)

Eadie, J. W., 'The development of Roman mailed cavalry', *Journal of Roman Studies* LVII (1967) 161-173

Ferri, S., *Arte Romana sul Danubio* (Milan 1933)

Florescu, F. B., *Tropaeum Traiani. Das Siegendenkmals von Adamklissi* (Bucharest-Bonn 1965)

Forni, G., *Il reclutamento delle legioni da Augusto a Diocleziano* (Milan 1953)

Furtwängler, A., 'Zum Tropaeum von Adamklissi', *Sitzungsberichte d. philosoph.-philolog.u.histor.Cl.d.k.bayer.Akad.Wiss.München* III (1904) 383

Homo, L., *Le siècle d'or de l'Empire Romain (Les Antonins)* (2nd ed. Paris 1969)

Lehmann-Hartleben, K., *Die Trajanssäule. Ein römisches Kunstwerk zu Beginn der Spätantike* (Berlin-Leipzig 1926)

Levi, A., and Levi, M., *Itineraria picta* (Rome 1967)

Marsden, E. W., *Greek and Roman Artillery: historical development* (Oxford 1969)

Paribeni, R., *Optimus Princeps* vol. I (Messina 1926)

Parker, H., *The Roman Legions* (2nd ed. Cambridge 1961)

Passerini, A., *Le coorti pretorie* (Rome 1939)

'Legio' in *Dizionario epigrafico di Antichità Romane*, ed. E. de Ruggiero, IV, f.18–20 (Rome 1950)

Petersen, E., 'Nuovi risultati storici della interpretazione della Colonna Traiana in Roma', *Atti del Congresso Internazionale di Scienze Storiche, Roma* II (1905) 3

Picard, G. C., *Les trophées romains* (Paris 1957)

Poggioli, R., *Cantare le gesta di Igor* (Milan 1954); for interpretation see A. Lo Gatto *Storia della Russia* (Milan 1947)

Richmond, I. A., 'Trajan's Army on Trajan's Column', *Papers of the British School at Rome* XIII (1935) 1–40

'Adamklissi', *Papers of the British School at Rome* XXII (1967) 29–39

Rossi, L., 'Le insegne militari nella monetazione imperiale Romana da Augusto a Commodo', *Rivista Italiana di Numismatica* XIII (1965) 41–81

(a) 'A Hypothesis Concerning the Auxiliary Signa of the Roman Army under the Antonines', *Numismatic Circular* LXXIV (1966) 240–41

(b) 'L'exercitus nella Colonna Traiana. Criteri generali ed elementi nuovi di studio su legionari ed auxilia', *Epigraphica* XXVIII (1966) 150–55

(a) 'The Symbolism Related to *Disciplina* on Roman Imperial Coins and Monuments', *Numismatic Circular* LXXV (1967) 130–31

(b) 'La guardia pretoriana e Germanica nella monetazione Giulio-Claudia', *Rivista Italiana di Numismatica* XV (1967) 15–38

'The Representation on Trajan's Column of Trajan's Rock-Cut Road in Upper Moesia: the Emperor's Road to Glory', *Antiquaries Journal 48* (1968) 41–6

'Il corpo santiario dell'armata Romana nel medio impero', *Physis* 11 (1969)

Salmon, E. T., *A History of the Roman World 30 BC–AD 138* (London 1959)

Smallwood, E. M., *Documents Illustrating the Principles of Nerva, Trajan and Hadrian* (Cambridge 1966)

Starr, C. G., *The Roman Imperial Navy 31 BC–AD 324* (2nd ed. Cambridge 1960)

Tocilescu, G., 'Despre Monumentul de la Adamklissi si diferite paveri asupra originii lor', *Revista pentru istorie, archeologia si filologia 10* (1909) 87–105

Toynbee, J. M. C., *The Flavian Reliefs from the Palazzo della Cancelleria in Rome*, Charlton lecture *39* (Oxford 1957)

Watson, G. R., *The Roman Soldier* (London 1969)

Webster, G., *The Roman Imperial Army* (London 1969)

Yadin, Y., *Masada* (London 1966)

SOURCES OF ILLUSTRATIONS

All illustrations not otherwise credited are the author's own. 1 photo Mansell Collection; 2 photo Rijksmuseum van Oudheden, Leiden; 7, 8 photo Tony Morrison; 9 photo Osterreichische Nationalbibliothek, Vienna; 11, 12, 14, 16, 17, 19, 20 photo British Museum, courtesy the Trustees; 6, 22, 23, 24, 25, 26 photo Professor F. B. Florescu; 27, 28, 29 photo Vindonissa Museum, Brugg; 30 photo Allard Pierson Museum, The University, Amsterdam; 34, 35 photo Professors C. and H. Daicoviciu; illustration to Appendix D; photo courtesy University of Thessalonika, The Society for the Promotion of Roman Studies, and Dr M. Speidal.

INDEX

Page numbers in italic type indicate illustrations.

236